Brother to Brother

Black Men
Speak to
Young Black Men

Beth Johnson, Editor

TP THE TOWNSEND LIBRARY

BROTHER TO BROTHER
Black Men Talk to Young Black Men

TP **THE TOWNSEND LIBRARY**

For more titles in the Townsend Library,
visit our website: www.townsendpress.com

Photo credits:
Photographs of Topher Sanders, Joe Davis, and Elijah Anderson
provided by subjects
Photograph of Calvin Sims by Shannon McCollum
All other photographs by Beth Johnson

Townsend Press, Inc.
439 Kelley Drive
West Berlin, New Jersey 08091
cs@townsendpress.com

ISBN-13: 978-1-59194-178-1
ISBN-10: 1-59194-178-4

Library of Congress Control Number:
2008937880

CONTENTS

Introduction 1

Kenyon Whittington 5

Rod Sutton.............................. 17

Topher Sanders 29

Joe Davis............................... 43

Andre Coleman 57

Ray Jones 73

Calvin Sims 89

Elijah Anderson 105

Fluke Fluker 121

Joseph Marshall, Jr............... 135

Introduction

Ten men. On the surface, they have little in common. They include schoolteachers and community activists, a professional storyteller and a journalist. They live in cities as far separated as Philadelphia and Los Angeles, San Francisco and Atlanta. Some dropped out of high school; others graduated from prestigious universities. Some grew up in stable, supportive homes; some were abandoned as children. Some have been in trouble with the law; one works in law enforcement.

But these ten men share a bond that transcends their differences: Each is a Black man in America. Each in his own way has given careful thought to what it *means* to be a Black man in America. Each feels a deep concern for and obligation to the younger Black men growing up in America. And as a result, each enthusiastically agreed to contribute an essay to the book you are holding in your hands.

What we asked of these men was something like this: "Imagine a young Black man, probably in his mid-teens, living in Camden or Compton or Detroit or East St. Louis. He's a good kid, a smart kid. But you're worried about him. You can see that he's getting hit with a lot of the temptations and pressures that can pull a young man down. Maybe he doesn't have the kind of older men in his life that a young guy needs—old heads who can help him get some perspective on life. If you had a chance to talk to that young man, what would you say to him?" These ten essays are their responses.

In discussing their contributions to *Brother to Brother*, many of these men talked frankly about their desire to become part of a new kind of conversation about race in America—a conversation that would acknowledge past injustices, but not get bogged down in them; one that would recognize self-destructive behavior, but not let that become an excuse for despair. Many of them worry about a fatalistic attitude held by some of their younger Black brothers—an attitude that says that to be Black means to be poor, underemployed, and without hope. One contributor mentioned the pain he felt when a child he works with scornfully told him, "*You* aren't Black." "What that child meant," he said sadly, "is that I speak like an educated man, and that I dress like a professional man." Another contributor remarked that when he mentions his two children, he is often asked where the children live. "When I say, 'They live in my house with my wife and me,' that's considered surprising. Because, you know," he added sarcastically, "a Black man isn't supposed to be married to the mother of his children." Countless young people struggle with the fear that they will be accused of "acting white" if they take school seriously. In the words of one contributor, "We badly need a new definition of what it is to be authentically Black—a definition that isn't based on negative, self-destructive beliefs."

As this book went to print, a Black man, Senator Barack Obama, had been nominated as a major political party's candidate for president of the United States. However the election turns out, this is a historic moment for our country. Millions of Americans of every race have been uplifted by the story of a Black man who both is proud of his race and refuses to be limited by any notion about what it means to be "really Black." In the same way, each of the ten proudly Black authors of this book has refused to limit his potential, hide his talents, or otherwise live his life according to anyone else's idea of what it meant to be authentically Black. Just as the story of Barack Obama has challenged and inspired a country, may the words of these ten men challenge and inspire you.

Kenyon Whittington

About Kenyon Whittington

Abandoned as a newborn, then briefly reclaimed by his abusive father and stepmother, Kenyon Whittington grew up in an atmosphere of fear, uncertainty, and neglect. His earliest memories are of moving between the homes of his violent father, his abusive and mentally unstable mother, and various foster families. Salvation arrived in the form of his grandmother and aunt, who eventually gained custody of the traumatized little boy and raised him as their own.

As he gradually overcame the horrors of his past, Kenyon became an outstanding student and the determined architect of his own path in life. He has consistently sought out positive opportunities, getting involved in activities ranging from debate and chess clubs to Upward Bound, Operation Understanding, and Philadelphia Futures. He is a graduate of Hampton University and is completing his master's degree in education at Holy Family University in Philadelphia. As a direct services coordinator of the Pennsylvania GEAR UP program, Kenyon helps middle-school and high-school students prepare for and succeed in college.

Kenyon Whittington Speaks

Hey young world, young world,
The future is in the palm of your hands.
Hey young world, young world,
Your destiny is at your command.
Believe what you want and achieve what you will,
But if it wasn't for you, tomorrow's day would
    stand still.
To be ignored is to lose your space,
So stand up, young world, and claim your place.
Don't just push yourselves to as far as you can see,
But strive towards your dreams, hopes, and most
    of all, victory.
Hey young world, young world,
Trouble will intervene with you.
But remember—young world, young world—
It is you that will bring you through.
Just like seeds from plants and trees,
That grow roots and sprout leaves,
You are the roots that hold things together,
While past generations like leaves fall in the weather.
Hey young world, young world, it's all on you,
You're like the hundredths of a second, seconds of a
    minute, minutes of an hour, that bring the days through.
Hey young world, young world,
Older generations are looking at you!
Please don't let them down, because life gives no rebounds.
You will fail not only them but most of all yourselves.
Hey young world, young world,
You mean the World,
Young World.

Hey there, my brothers. I want to talk with you about success—your success, and how you are going to achieve it.

Your vision of success may be different from mine. It's up to you to define it in your own way. But I'd like to argue that some things often seen as success are not it at all. Success cannot be measured by material things like cash, cars, and jewelry. Those are all things that can be ours one day and lost the next. True success can't be bought and can't be sold. Neither can its close relatives, integrity and respect. In my mind, success is about investing fully in the best part of yourself. It's about the values that you choose, live by, and pass on to future generations.

The values you choose don't have to be determined by your circumstances. Let me give you an example. I'll call him Person A. Person A shows up to school sometimes. He's usually late. He comes into class with a Zune or an iPod and his cell phone turned on. He's never prepared for class; he doesn't even have a pen or paper. Person A doesn't follow the school dress code; his pants sag below his waistline to display his underwear to the world. Sometimes Person A is rude to teachers. He intimidates and even fights other students.

Meanwhile, there's Person B. Person B is studious;

he shows up for class on time. He has the supplies he needs to be a successful student: pen, paper, books, and completed assignments. Person B helps build the community by being part of school activities. He shows self-respect through his appearance, and he shows respect for others through his behavior.

Person A and Person B are neighbors. They come from the same crime-infested housing project. They are both being raised by guardians who are not their biological parents. But Person B has decided to take charge of his future. Because his commitment to success is obvious, people around him want to help him along. They are drawn to investing in that young man's future. Person A, however, shows disregard for himself and those around him. He doesn't seem invested in his own future. Seeing that, fewer people invest in him. Unlike Person B, he has not developed credibility with those around him. All he has built is a negative reputation.

The good news is that someone like Person A can choose a new path to travel. Despite what all the other Person A's around him are doing, he can make different choices for his own life. Like Person B, he can choose to be an individual making positive choices for his future.

It's hard to choose a pathway in life until you have a value system in place. Do *you*? What do *you* value? Question yourself. Does your value system lift you and the world up, or bring you down? Your list of values can be short or long. Mine, for instance, includes love, peace, and respect. The important thing is that you know them and are loyal to them. They will guide you as you find your own destiny.

But to succeed in any terms, you must value learning. More than any single thing, leaning is essential to your progress through life's journey. To deny a person—to deny yourself—a proper education is to deny that person pride, self-esteem, and self-reliance. An uneducated person is, in a sense, crippled to the level of a slave. While people are surely going to fail you in life, you can rise above anything if you refuse to fail yourself.

Besides defining success and establishing your values, a third thing I'd like to encourage you to do is to work hard to build community. The concerns and issues you face are not yours alone. They are shared by your brothers. Together you have far greater strength than you do individually; together you can face the enemies that are waiting to bring you down. And the greatest enemy of all is ignorance. Ignorance thrives on fear and isolation. Ignorance can be any aspect of your life— yourself, your family, your friends—that prevents you from being the absolute best that you can be. Ignorance is any individual, institution, or code of behavior that prevents you from moving forward. But ignorance has power only if you choose to embrace it and refuse to proclaim a brighter future. By joining together with other young brothers, with your neighbors, with your larger community, you can uplift yourself and everyone around you. You can build a community that works in unison and thrives on positivity. Everyone can be a leader in this kind of community, because it's not about who can think the fastest, but how collectively you can think the furthest. Collectively, you can create a vision of your common future.

You might be asking, "So why should I listen to what you have to say? You don't know what kind of obstacles I face in my life. You're talking about a fantasy world. In the real world, with real problems, dreams don't come true."

I hear you. You deserve to know where I'm coming from with all this. In response, I want to tell you about a young man who is a living example of everything I have said. He's a man who, according to every indicator, should be another sad statistic. Instead, his life illustrates the possibility of success.

Strike one—as a baby, this young man was first abused, then abandoned, by his biological parents. In consequence, he spent the most delicate years of his life traveling from foster home to foster home. A brief reunion with his parents was punctuated by emotional, psychological, and physical torture before he was rescued by his grandmother and aunt.

Strike two—his grandmother died. Without the woman he most loved and depended upon, he was once again adrift, with no anchor in his life. Looking around him for direction, he saw negative peer pressure, drugs and gangs, and all the other daily realities of life in the projects.

Strike three—he was a Black man in America. Like many of his brothers, he felt the pressures of racism bearing down on him, the negative expectations that society held for him. He would fail, that society said. He would not live to see 21.

Three strikes and the world said, "You're out."

"No, I am not!" he replied. "My life is no ballgame. In God's eyes, I am never out."

Yes, he was born a victim of grim circumstances. He faced great adversity and many obstacles in the pursuit of his dreams. But he held fast to those dreams and never wavered. He chose to be a victor and never a victim. He refused to use adversity as an excuse for failure.

I know this man well. He is me. I have dreamed what some might call the impossible dream, but to me there is no impossibility. I chose, and continue to choose, to put forth my best effort and reap the consequences of my actions.

As long as it is done from the heart, it is worth doing.

It's not about cars or cash or jewelry.

It's not about being #1 or #100.

It's not about scoring 2400 or 400 on the SAT.

It's not about being in the elite honors class or in a remedial course.

Because none of these things can show who you are inside your heart.

Whether you move on to a trade school, the working world, the military, a community college, or a university, what matters is what you do while you are there. No two of us have identical strengths and weaknesses. What is important is that we know ourselves, using our strengths and striving to improve ourselves. When we need encouragement, we can look at inspiring historical figures like W.E.B. DuBois and Malcolm X. One was a scholar, one was a convict; but both became prominent, positive role models in the African American community.

Me? Today I am working full time for the Philadelphia School District's GEAR UP program. There I help guide young people to become college-aware and prepared for college success. I'm also close to completing course work at Holy Family University for my master's degree in elementary education.

The statistics say none of this should be true.

I say statistics are only numbers.

We have the power to create lives we can be proud of. We can take life's roadblocks and turn them into stepping stones.

What will you do to stay true to your dreams and to make them a magnificent reality?

Rod Sutton

About Rod Sutton

As a 200-pound thirteen-year-old, Rod Sutton was a well-known figure in his middle school. It wasn't only his size that made him stand out; it was his attitude. During his years in elementary school, Rod had been suspended fifty-two times. Finally, after assaulting a teacher, Rod was permanently expelled from his school district. That's when St. Benedict's School, a school run by Catholic monks in Newark, New Jersey, agreed to accept Rod on a trial basis.

Two weeks after his arrival at the school, Rod got into a fight with another student that ended with several classroom windows being shattered. Rod was certain he would be kicked out of St. Benedict's. Instead, the headmaster gently told him, "I don't believe in children missing school. You're going to be something great someday. Now go sweep up that glass."

That day marked a turning point for Rod. He graduated from St. Benedict's and went on to earn a sociology degree from Franklin and Marshall College in Lancaster, Pennsylvania. Later, as a teacher in the Camden, New Jersey, school district, he developed an innovative program called "Urban Males" to help fifth-grade boys stay on track academically and personally. Today Rod teaches in the Philadelphia public schools.

He and his wife Jean are the parents of a daughter and a son.

Rod Sutton Speaks

We African American males are in trouble. Particularly *young* African American males. As a group, we occupy the bottom rung of the American social ladder. We die the youngest. We have the worst health problems. We are the most likely to be imprisoned. We have the poorest school records. We are most likely to be both the perpetrators and the victims of violent crime.

It is rare to see an African American man on a college campus or working in a business environment or in any positive professional capacity outside of entertainment or professional sports. Apart from entertainment or sports, the only places you will find significant numbers of Black brothers are in prisons, on the deadly inner-city street corners, and sadly, in the morgue and graveyards.

How did we get here? And what can we do?

In answer to "how did we get here," I think of Kanye West's words in his rap song "Jesus Walks." Kanye says, "Yo, we're at war. We're at war with terrorism, racism, and most of all we're at war with ourselves." Tragically, Kanye is right. We Black males are killing each other. And when we are not physically hurting one another, we are making choices that keep us at the bottom.

We pull each other down with the image of ourselves that we choose to embrace. Many of the current generation of young Black men define themselves as "niggas." As an inner-city educator and a brother from the hood, I can't tell you how many young men have told me that we Black men are niggas. And they tell me this in a way that indicates they are either proud of placing themselves in an inferior position, or else they don't understand the history of the word "nigga" and how offensive it is.

But calling themselves "niggas" reflects the social world that these young Black men have created. It's a world based on negative stereotypes and negative thinking. Being a nigga is all about what you DON'T do. A nigga doesn't dress in clothes that fit properly. A nigga doesn't speak correct English. A nigga doesn't enjoy learning. A nigga doesn't find one girl to love and care for and build a lasting relationship with. A nigga doesn't plan to marry and raise a family. A nigga doesn't aspire to be anything but a thug or a hood rat.

A brother who dares to try to separate himself from this negativity is put down. If he tries to be something more than a nigga, he is mocked as acting "white" or "soft" or "sweet." Each of these names is meant to demean a young Black male, make him feel less than a man. It is meant to punish him for trying to be something more. We brothers are like a barrel of crabs. One of us tries to crawl out to sunlight and freedom, and the others are pulling him back in. We're acting out Kanye's lyric: "Most of all, we're at war with ourselves."

Ever since the Black man came to America, each generation has struggled with the negative effect the word "nigga" has had on the self-esteem of young brothers. But my generation was the first to turn it into a term of affection or even a badge of ability. To be a nigga meant that you could handle yourself on the street.

I remember the day that I embraced my identity as a nigga. I was 16. My home streets of Newark, New Jersey, were as mean and cruel as they are today. As a young Black male, I knew I would be tested daily. I had to stick with people who I could trust and who I knew would have my back. During these years on the streets, I formed some of the strongest friendships imaginable. Because we knew that we were in a life-and-death struggle every time we chose to leave our homes, we formed bonds that were as close as family ties.

The first order of business was that you couldn't appear soft or weak in any way. This was especially important for me because I was big. When anyone encountered our posse, I was the first person they sized up. They'd think, "If I can take down the Big Boy, we can handle the rest." As a result, I felt the need to never, ever take an ass-whupping. I quickly developed the habit of hitting first. I didn't talk much. If I felt violated, I came in swinging. And it was pretty easy to violate me. Just use the wrong tone of voice.

On this day, my cousin had just stolen a case of beer from the Pabst brewery. He and his crew had been around the corner when another guy, Khalid, got into a fight with my cousin over a girl. Soon my cousin came up my street, bleeding from the mouth, saying, "That nigga Khalid hit me." I ran around the corner to where Khalid was still sitting on the corner. I was a big kid, but Khalid was five years older, 6 foot 5, and weighed 230 pounds, so I figured I needed to disable him quick. I picked up a beer bottle and busted it over his head, putting him into a daze. I then grabbed him and slammed him head-first into the brick wall of the neighboring building. Then I proceeded to give him a beating. Through it all I could hear girls screaming that I was going to kill him. I didn't stop until somebody's mother threatened to call the cops.

Brother to Brother

So the next day, I was walking down the street and an old head named Wadou, just out of prison, called out to me. He said, "I just saw Khalid with a mouth full of blood. Did you do that?" I smirked and nodded, proud as a peacock. Wadou told me, "I am going to call you 'Brass'—short for "brass knuckles." Wow! I had effectively handled my business on the streets of Newark. At 16, I felt I was one of the biggest, baddest niggas around. I had respect, as it was defined in my neighborhood.

But a few days after Wadou spoke to me, another old head from the neighborhood saw me hanging around. His name was Eric. He was a lawyer who worked on Wall Street. He didn't congratulate me on my street brawl. Instead he said, "Eventually you're going to have to grow up and leave all of this bullshit behind. You're a smart kid. If you take control of your life, you could write your own ticket out of here."

This wasn't the first time I'd heard words like this. My biological father used to tell me similar things. Before he died, he would tell my mom, "Rod is my investment. He is going to be something one day." Years later, I would see how frustrated my stepfather, David Sutton, would get with me. He could see that I had potential that I wasn't using. And, of course, my mother prayed for my success every day.

I understood my parents' concern. But I didn't think they fully understood the daily threat of the streets. I knew that the streets of Newark could spring death on a Black male—usually at the hands of another Black male—at any moment. By creating a reputation as a bad nigga, I hoped to protect myself. But I knew that my time was running out. I had been very fortunate so far, meaning that I had neither been killed or killed anybody myself. But it was just a matter of time. Before long, I would have to choose the path of Wadou or of Eric.

I chose Eric's. But until I could leave where I was living, I realized I was going to have to learn to live in two worlds at once. I was going to have to learn to do what they call "code switching." In certain settings, I would have to conceal my book smarts. In others, I would have to hide my street smarts. At times, I thought this split would rip me apart. I never felt comfortable in any setting, never felt that I could show anybody who I really was. I knew the streets weren't the place for me, because I wanted a better life for myself. But we brothers have done a magnificent job of convincing mainstream America that we are bad niggas and not to be messed with. As a result, even when I no longer wanted to play this role, the stereotype was assigned to me anyway. Everywhere I went, I felt suspicion and discomfort around me. I believe that this constant mental tug-of-war contributes to the struggle with alcohol that I am dealing with today.

When a brother decides to separate himself from the streets and tries to live a better life, he finds himself in a lonely place. As he moves into the mainstream, he can find nothing to connect him to the world where he grew up. And once he is in the mainstream, he is no longer welcome back in his original world. This is the challenge the Black man faces as he tries to make his way out of the hood—he is viewed with suspicion in both worlds.

How have I coped with this dilemma? First, I found a woman who I could build a life with and start a family. She helped me make the transition from being a nigga to being a man. Secondly, I began listening to older African American men who had experienced what I was going through. As they say, "There is nothing new under the sun." These older men had stood where I was standing and knew how it felt. Through them, I began to think more about the positive male role models I had known. I thought about my deceased father and the unconditional love he had for his family. I thought of my stepdad and his commitment to duty and honor. I thought of my late uncles, one a principal of a New Jersey school and the other a corrections officer. And I thought, of course, of Eric.

In addition, I joined a church. This was important for a number of reasons. First, it strengthened my faith for the still difficult road that lay ahead. (Just because you're out of the hood doesn't mean the hard work is over.) In addition, it put me in constant contact with responsible, committed Black men who have a positive image of themselves and of me. The church also provides a community that keeps me accountable and on the right track.

Throughout it all, I have learned to accept the help of kind-hearted individuals who wanted to help me succeed in the mainstream. This has included elementary, junior-high, and high-school teachers; college professors and administrators; and a host of other caring human beings that God placed in my path at the right moment to gently (and sometimes not so gently) push me in the right direction.

Lastly and most importantly, I found a purpose. I dedicated myself to the memory of those brothers who, by choice or by fate, didn't make it out. I honor them by trying to help as many young brothers as possible escape the death trap of the streets.

Topher Sanders

About Topher Sanders

Topher Sanders is a former officer in the United States Air Force. In that profession, he was following in the footsteps of his mother, Jackie, a twenty-year Air Force veteran. A military brat, Topher was born in Italy and lived in Florida, Georgia, Hawaii, and Alabama throughout his mother's military career.

Despite the challenges of being a single mother, Jackie gave Topher a strong sense of personal responsibility by making him turn tough moments into learning lessons. The death of a friend's mother, described in the essay that follows, led to one such important lesson. Topher wrote an account of the incident that was published in *Newsweek* magazine.

When Topher left the military, he started freelance writing for magazines and newspapers before eventually landing a full-time job as a journalist with a paper in Montgomery, Alabama.

Topher now lives in Jacksonville, Florida, with his wife. He is an education reporter for the *Florida Times-Union* and is working with a co-author on his first book.

Topher Sanders Speaks

As I watched my grandfather's casket being lowered into the ground, I looked at the faces of the men around me. Just as I expected, none of them were crying. I found myself mimicking what I saw around me. Not a single tear ran down my cheek.

But these other men hadn't lost their grandfather. I had. My grandfather deserved my tears, but my misunderstanding of what it meant to be a man prevented them from flowing.

I was 13. I stood by his grave with a dry, hard face, like the kind I had seen on hip-hop artists like Tupac Shakur and actors like Denzel Washington.

My grandfather was the only man in my family that I had spent significant time with. He taught me how to clean and prepare fresh fish for cooking and how to play checkers and card games. During the summers when I would visit my grandparents in Columbus, Georgia, he and I would sit on their porch and eat sausage sandwiches and talk about life and sports. He was an avid San Francisco 49ers fan and gave me my love for the game by rooting for Jerry Rice and Joe Montana.

Yet, with all that he had taught me and done for me, I didn't shed one tear when my grandfather died.

Topher Sanders

I thought I wasn't supposed to.

My mother cried, of course, but she was supposed to cry. She was a woman. But I was becoming a man, and men don't cry. I was supposed to be strong, and tears are not a show of strength.

We Black men learn quickly as we're growing up that to get the respect of our peers, we have to be hard. Being hard means you don't flinch at life. You sure don't cry. The streets we walk on, the movies we watch, and the music we listen to all teach us that men who cry are weak. And the weak get tried.

So we build a wall that keeps us from feeling all the things that would otherwise hit our hearts and make us feel pain.

But what does it really mean to be a man? How does a man really deal with emotions?

For a long time I thought manhood meant holding in my emotions and never showing my vulnerability. When you don't have examples of manhood in your own home, you pull those examples from the neighborhood or from television and music. Popular culture constantly exaggerates the masculinity of Black men. According to that culture, Black men are the hardest creatures on Earth. We are constantly portrayed as remorseless killers and uncaring fathers. Whether it's Tupac, Ice Cube,

Larenz Tate, or even younger artists like Plies and Uncle Murda, the image of Black men is consistent.

In the 1991 movie *Boyz n the Hood*, when the character Ricky dies, Ice Cube's character, Doughboy, doesn't shed a tear for his own brother. Instead he seeks revenge with Ricky's blood still on his clothes.

Along with my friends, I consumed those images and many more. We all swallowed the same message—Black men are hard. Only the weak show their emotions. Off the movie screen, in our own Montgomery, Alabama, neighborhood, the message was repeated again and again. If a kid was ever on the losing end of a fight in my neighborhood, he'd better hold onto those tears until he got home or he would forever be marked as a buster or a coward. Responding to all these messages, we developed an outer shell, like turtles. That shell stayed hard on the outside so nobody could ever penetrate it and hurt us.

I spent my teenage years trying to prove to other Black men in my school and neighborhood that I was to be respected and not to be tested. I was sure I would lose all respect with my peers if I cried openly about anything.

And then there was my grandfather. I remember so distinctly the day when the family dog, Brisco, was killed. I was 6 at the time. My grandfather was crossing the street, and Brisco ran into the road to follow him. A car hit him. My grandfather carried his beloved dog home and placed his body on the porch.

Brisco had been a member of the family since my mother was in high school. He was getting old, but he still had enough energy to play with me and follow my grandfather around for errands. My grandmother was beside herself with weeping, but my grandfather didn't cry. "He died in my arms," he kept saying. It was obvious that he was deeply grieved by the dog's loss. But he didn't shed a tear. Watching my grandfather deal with Brisco's death gave me an early example of how men deal—or don't deal—with grief.

It took the loss of my good friend's mother to show me that emotion and tears can be one of the healthiest things for a man to experience.

His name was Ronald, and he was my boy. He lived right next door, and we hung out all the time. He was a little bit younger than me, so while we were friends, I was also his mentor in some ways. We got in trouble together, pursued girls together, and had a few altercations in the streets together. We were tight.

We would become even tighter.

When I got home from school one day, my mother

told me that Ronald's mother had suddenly died. I was 15 and Ronald was 13.

The news hit me like a NFL linebacker. I was shaking, and I didn't know what to do.

"He wants you to go see him," my mother said.

He wants to see me? I thought. Why? What can I do?

I went to my room and paced around in circles, thinking about what I would say or do. I started making phone calls to our friends. It was hard being the first of our circle of friends to know the news. I dreaded saying the words.

"Ronald's mom died," I said to Trevor, the first friend I reached.

"Are you serious, man?" Trevor said. He wasn't really asking a question. He was trying to convince himself of the reality.

I got in touch with all of our friends. They all said they would come right over.

I knew that alerting our friends was the right thing to do, but there was another reason I called them. I didn't want to face Ronald alone. I had no idea how to comfort my friend, and I was scared.

I eventually mustered up the courage to head over to Ronald's house. He lived right next door, but the walk across our yards was the longest in my life.

When I got to the front door of Ronald's home, I stared at the doorbell for several seconds. I was terrified of the emotions that were going to be inside that house.

I rang the doorbell. Ronald's older brother, Adrian, opened the door. His eyes were red and swollen, and he wouldn't look directly at me. Adrian was one of the hardest kids in the neighborhood, but today he looked vulnerable and scared.

"Ronald's in the living room," he said.

I could hear sniffles and sobs coming from around the corner. When I walked into the living room, Ronald was on the couch. He was gripping a pillow to his chest and moaning in pain. Tears streamed down his face as he rocked back and forth.

I sat beside him and awkwardly patted his shoulder. Through his tears, he asked me, "Why, Topher? Why my mom?"

I could only shake my head and say, "I don't know, Ron, I don't know."

As I witnessed the pain on his face, I began to feel the tears sting my own eyes. I tightened my face, but the tears flowed anyway. I reached for Ronald and put my arms around him. He hugged me back. When our friends arrived, they found us holding each other, rocking back and forth and crying together. One by one our friends joined us in our huddle of tears. We all cried together for our friend and his mother.

What happened that day at Ronald's house was a significant event in my life. When I looked at my friend and the tears pouring from his eyes, I couldn't hold onto the hardness that I was developing in every other aspect of my life. As a hard, cold man, I couldn't offer anything to Ronald. As a caring friend, I could share his grief and maybe lessen it a little.

When we all left Ronald's house, we gave each other some dap and returned to our homes. Once I was alone in my room, I sat on my bed and let out a big breath. Crying with Ronald and for Ronald's loss seemed like one of the realest things I had done in my young life. I felt strangely free. Before going to Ronald's house, I felt a terrible tightness in my chest. But expressing my pain with Ronald was like someone had turned a knob inside me and released tons of pressure.

After that day, my friends and I developed a different level of friendship. There was a closeness between us that had not existed before. We had seen each other at our most vulnerable, yet we weren't judging each other for it. In fact, we all gained a bit more respect for each other than we had before we walked into Ronald's house. We asked about each other's families more and were more conscious of Ronald's emotions in the years after his mom passed. Her death forced us to be more considerate and thoughtful. I no longer felt the need to put on airs in front of this group of young men. The change wasn't instant, but eventually, it bled into my dealings with other people.

That day at Ronald's house, I let go of my false ideas about manhood and embraced another side of manhood, one that is necessary for healthy men. I realized that tears aren't an enemy of masculinity. I learned that a real man is understanding and caring toward the people he loves. Being hard all the time doesn't allow a man to show that he cares for someone. And sometimes caring for someone means you cry with them or for them.

Acting hard all the time will cripple you emotionally. It will prevent you from building and maintaining positive relationships with women. It will keep you from developing true friendships. It will force you to place impossible standards on your children when you have them.

All of the most important relationships in your life will revolve around emotions and honesty. When you prevent people from seeing your emotional side, you prevent them from truly getting to know you. That will eventually kill any relationship—whether it's with friends or girlfriends. When you are constantly acting harder than the next guy, you push away your own emotions, and you dismiss the emotions of others. When I was in high school, there were girls who were interested in me and reached out to me, but nothing genuine ever developed because I never responded to their emotions. Instead I acted like their feelings didn't matter and that I was too cool and hard to care.

Holding back your emotions seems like a great way to be to protect yourself from being hurt, but over time, it is guaranteed to kill your friendships and romantic connections. You can't form genuine bonds with people when you're constantly masking or suppressing your emotions. All of that emotion you bottle up inside you begins to eat away at the very qualities that can make you a good friend, husband, and father. Qualities like sensitivity, caring and love are sacrificed to maintain that rough exterior. Over time you become mean and unhappy, and all for the sake of being one of the baddest dudes in the neighborhood.

What you lose just isn't worth it.

The respect the neighborhood shows you for being

the hardest cat on the block fades with time. The older you get, the less people respect the hard tough guy. Eventually there will be a younger and tougher guy coming to replace you. But if you develop warm and genuine relationships with friends and family, you've got something that will only grow stronger and richer with time. I won't lie—positive relationships built on honesty and freely flowing emotions are sometimes hard. They take time to maintain. But the payoff is well worth the effort.

I lost the chance to be real about how painful it was to lose my grandfather. Instead, I let my image of what I thought a man was keep me from being honest at my grandfather's funeral.

I reclaimed that honesty when Ronald's mother died. It was hard to deal with, and it was painful, but it was worth it to be there for my friend and to support him in his time of sorrow. I began to learn that day that tears are not a sign of weakness. They can be a sign of strength—true strength, not some act that we put on for others' benefit.

Today I am a writer, and I spend much of my time exploring my emotions and the emotions of others. Honestly, I am only able to be the kind of writer I am because of my willingness to express my emotions:

happiness, sadness and everything in between. As I've grown older, I've developer stronger bonds with my friends and family. I am married to a wonderful woman who loves me and who I love. Our relationship is filled with strong and positive emotions that I have to confront and deal with every day. It isn't always easy, but by working together, we help each other become better people. I wouldn't have been able to develop this kind of relationship had I not learned the lesson taught to me when Ronald lost his mother. My wife and I don't have any kids yet, but when we do, I hope I'm able to raise a strong, intelligent son who isn't afraid to cry.

Joe Davis

About Joe Davis

Joe Davis tells people, "If I had not gotten shot, I would be dead today." By the time Joe was 14, he was drinking and using marijuana. At 16, he had moved on to cocaine and pills. By 25, he was a heroin addict and drug dealer. That same year, he was shot in the back by the boyfriend of a girl he'd argued with. After eight months in the hospital, Joe was released in a wheelchair, paralyzed from the chest down. He went back to selling drugs, spiraling even further downward into addiction and health problems, until he attempted suicide by swallowing a bottle of pills. He awoke from a coma determined to clean up his life and seek forgiveness from the people he had wronged.

Since then, Joe has earned an associate's degree from community college, a bachelor's degree in mental health, and a master's degree in social work from the University of Pennsylvania. He is coordinator of Think First, a violence-prevention program operated by Magee Rehabilitation Hospital in Philadelphia. In his free time, Joe travels to high schools and youth groups, taking every opportunity to speak with young people about his life, hoping to turn them away from the dead-end path he once traveled. With the support of his wife

Terri, Joe has dedicated his life to turning others away from the way of violence and death.

Joe Davis Speaks

I have spent much of the past fifteen years speaking to young Black men like yourselves. When I'm speaking in schools or community organizations or correctional facilities, I see hundreds and hundreds of young brothers like you who have been left behind, and who will continue to be left behind. And for the most part, if you are left behind, it will be your own fault.

"My own fault?" you might say. "Fool, you ought to see where I come from. You ought to see what I've grown up with. I never had a chance. I had to get my hustle on the best way I know."

But I'm telling you, I've seen just about every set of circumstances you could tell me about. I'm still telling you that you have a choice what to do about those circumstances. And yes, it'll be your fault if you buy the bill of goods that so many people are eager to sell you. They'll tell you that slinging dope in your own community is cool. Your own community—the one where your mothers and grandmothers sit on the porch, and where your brothers and sisters and children play. They'll tell you to close your eyes to those people and do your piece of damage to your own community, trying to be a big balla.

I know what I'm talking about. I slung for a minute and made a few bucks. What I won from that was a few gun charges, a few drug cases, and one short bit in the joint. What I lost was just about everything— my self-respect, my family's trust, my health, and nearly my life.

If you still decide to get your hustle on, let me tell you what you have to look forward to. Once you get a package, you're responsible for it. You can sell it, you can use it, or you can give it away, but when it comes time to give that money up, you better have it. You pay up or you die. If you have the money, then you have to get a hammer to protect it from the stick-up boys who are trying to get their hustle on, just like you. And if you don't have it, before you die you might have the pleasure of seeing your house burned down or your sister raped multiple times to remind you to pay your debt.

Maybe you think that selling dope or being a stick-up thug will get you respect. I understand how it feels to want respect. When I was in the fifth and sixth grades, I was a poor reader. I was embarrassed when the teacher would ask me to read out loud, and I'd try to come up with excuses. I knew if I did read, other kids would laugh at me. Then I'd get angry and start a fight. You know, to get myself some respect. I dropped out of school in tenth grade and drifted into the military—a traditional way out of the hood for many Black men. Only not for me. I had no discipline, no self-respect, even though I thought I could demand respect from others. I went in, got through boot camp, and was stationed in Okinawa, Japan. I lasted for three months before I got into a fight. I don't even remember what was behind the fight, but I was thrown in the brig for three months. Once I got out, all I wanted to do was party, and that's what I did until the military got sick of me and kicked me to the curb.

When I came home, I was like a mad dog. I remember my dad telling me, "If a man doesn't work, he'll steal." And I wasn't interested in work. Still no discipline; no self-respect. My dad was right. I stole everything that wasn't nailed down. I didn't realize yet that I had a drug habit. I still told myself that I just liked getting high. But I was lying to myself. My every waking hour was about drug culture. That included stealing, lying, selling, and using.

I was 25—still young. One day I was getting high

in the house where I sold drugs. A young girl lived there. She was a strange girl who would do things like jump out windows or cut herself. Years later she was continuing to do these crazy things as well as have a lot of unprotected sex that produced a lot of children she could not care for. I realize now she had a mental illness. Anyway, on this particular day she was disturbing me, coming into the room where I was getting my fix. I told her to get out, threatened her. She told her fourteen-year-old boyfriend to shoot me. He did it.

When the bullet ripped into me, I fell into the street and my teeth drove through my lips. I tried to crawl under a car because I didn't know if that young boy with a gun was still there. As I lay there in the street like a pile of garbage, I heard my mom screaming, "Oh no; not my baby; not my baby!" The cops came and picked me up by the back of the collar and my belt loops and threw me in the back of the wagon. I heard another cop say, "Somebody finally got that nigger." I thought I was being slick, slinging dope in my neighborhood, being a thief and a junkie. But I was just a small turd in a toilet where everything stank.

In the hospital, as they were tearing my clothes off, I heard a doc say, "Oh, we got another one." A Black man with a bullet in him is so common that the folks who have to care for us don't see it as a critical event. For that matter, neither do we. If a Black child is killed, it may be a top news story at 6 o'clock, but by 11 that same child gets just a small mention. So the next morning when the doctors came into my room and said I was going to be a T-3 paraplegic and probably crippled for the rest of my life, I was already old news.

That night, all alone in my hospital room, I cried a river of tears. You name the reason, I cried for it. I cried because I was crippled. I cried because I was a junkie with no future. I cried because I was stupid and Black. Yeah, stupid and Black. I put that in because race matters. There's a thing called "white privilege," and it's real, and it's a problem. But as a race of people, you and I have been focused on what somebody white did to us. The fact is, nobody white made me sell dope. Nobody white made me turn my back on education. Nobody white made me get thrown out of the military. And ain't nobody white going to fix us. That job will be up to us.

I got out of the hospital. I went back to the same house and began selling dope again, because it's all I knew how to do. But I was crippled, a wounded animal there in the jungle. They say "there is no honor among thieves," and they are right. My brothers swooped down on me like I was a hunk of fresh meat. They beat me and took my money and dope. I had to stop slinging and depend on my social security check. I already felt like crap because I wasn't what I used to be, and now I was living in poverty. Like a damn slave, I had to depend on a handout. My dad is 73 and has worked his entire life. Once—just once—he was laid off and had to apply for public assistance. That was the only time my family was ever on welfare. Dad told me later that going to that office was the most humiliating experience of his life. And now, welfare is a way of life for many of us.

After I got beat up a few times, Mom let me come home to live. Dad never would have allowed it, but she just did it without telling him. To show my "appreciation," I sold dope out of their house. Like a fool, I thought I could control the game. Of course, there was only the illusion of control. Those addicts would have rolled on my mom just as fast as they would have rolled on me. Luckily, that didn't happen.

But one night I was upstairs in the back room, getting high like junkies do, and I decided I didn't want to live anymore. That's where cocaine takes you eventually. When you smoke it, you have a few moments of complete happiness, but then the dope is gone, and you plunge into depression. My thought was to take a bunch of pills and wait until I got drowsy. Then I was going to light a cigarette, smoke it down, and let it fall on the mattress. I was going to take my whole family with me—my mother, father, two sisters, and brother. The dope had made me that crazy.

It didn't work out that way. The cigarette went out, my sister heard me choking, and I woke up in the hospital two days later with my mom sitting by my bed, stroking my hair. She and I had a long talk there in the hospital, with her telling me how much she wanted to see me straight again before she died. I asked her if she would help me, and she said yes.

For the next solid year, my mom helped me. She was like a soldier. She stood at the front door to keep away unwanted visitors. She blocked phone calls so that I would not talk to anyone who might help me get high. She did what I was not yet strong enough to do for myself. And in that upstairs bedroom, I began to believe that I did not have to get high to be somebody. I began eating normally, sleeping at regular hours. Eventually I ventured out onto the street, not for any madness, but to find a job. I was tired of being a slave. I wanted to be a free man, in charge of my own destiny. And I did find a job, and thirteen years later I had earned a master's degree in social work from the University of Pennsylvania. It was hard; I'm not going to tell you it wasn't. I'm still not an academic guy. I sometimes have to read a book three times, and even then I don't get it all. So I humble myself and ask for help, just like I asked my mom to help me all those years ago. I've found that there are some really cool people in the world who thrive on helping others. And now, I am one of them.

My mother died recently in my home. After all I'd put her through, she died with the satisfaction of knowing that her boy was clean. I can't tell you what it means to me to be able to tell you that.

There's nothing anybody can tell me about how great dope is. It's fun until it's not fun, and then it ruins your life. And you don't have to live that life. I don't care what your circumstances are. I know for a fact that some of you come from nasty places. Maybe dope is sold out of your home. Maybe your mom has a new boyfriend who doesn't like you, so he hits you every chance he gets. Maybe your mom is called a bitch so often she thinks that's her name. Maybe you've been introduced to sex already, and not in a way that you wanted. Maybe your home is hot in the summer and freezing in the winter. Maybe you get high with your own parents. But your past does not have to be your future. You do not have to become what your parents are because you see them smoke dope. You don't have to become an addict because your mom is turning tricks. You don't have to treat women like dirt. I know it is difficult to walk a straight road when everyone around you seems crooked. But it can be done.

I know that for many of you, no one has ever told you that you are worthy, that you are capable, that you can be better, no matter what your circumstances are. Let me be the guy who tells you. You are capable. You can be better. I am asking you—no, I'm begging you—hold on and do the right thing. Stay off the dope. Stay in school. Take it seriously. Study, study, study. I know that is a hard pill to swallow when it feels like someone has a foot on your neck, but I swear to you, it is your way to a better life. If you turn your back on education, you resign yourself to a life of poverty and dependence.

If your friends are holding you back, get some new friends. Read every day. Write something every day. If you are in a place where reading and writing are frowned upon, find yourself a place where they are not. If you hear criticism, if people say, "You think you're better than us?"—know for sure that those people want you to fail, because that makes them feel better about themselves. Do not let their failures be your destiny. You can do better.

Brothers, if no one else has told you that they love you, let me be the one. I love you. Join with me in becoming part of our community's solution, not part of the problem.

Andre Coleman

About Andre Coleman

Andre Coleman was born in 1973 in Philadelphia. He was the youngest of seven children, all of whom soon became wards of Baptist Children's Services and were raised in a group home. After having been born into an environment of poverty and neglect, Andre was forced to deal with the instability of life in foster care.

Andre's discovery that he could succeed in school gave him an anchor in life. As a leader of his school's safety patrol, an active participant at the West Philadelphia Community Center, and a member of Drexel University's "Pre-Bound" program, Andre found that he could leave the bleak realities of his life behind and create a bright future. An unexpected event in his teens threatened to pull Andre off his positive path in life, but after a few stumbles, he regained his footing. Andre attended Penn State University and is a certified emergency medical technician. He works as a corrections officer at Chester County Prison in Pennsylvania, where he is a training officer and a member of the honor guard. He is serving his second term as a member of the board of Baptist Children's Services, the organization that provided foster care for him and his siblings. Andre and his fiancée live in Wilmington, Delaware.

Andre Coleman Speaks

My first memories are of living in a pink house in southwest Philadelphia. I was the youngest of seven brothers and sisters. The oldest was 11, and I was 2. I don't remember any adults being there. I don't know how we lived. I don't know if the older ones went to school. I guess someone must have come by with food for us from time to time. The oldest girls sort of watched over the rest of us.

One day my older brother was sliding down the banister. When I tried to follow him, I fell and broke my leg. At the hospital, the doctors discovered I had hepatitis, an infectious liver disease. They wanted my brothers and sisters tested to see if they had it too, so they called the Department of Human Services and told them to go to the house. DHS sent some people out there, and they saw how we were living. They got quite a shock. From what they tell me, the social workers were coming out of there in tears. The worst thing was, there wasn't any running water, so we'd been using the bathtub as a toilet. That gives you some idea of what this house was like.

All seven of us were infected with hepatitis. They took us to Philadelphia General Hospital, where we were given a separate wing to keep us away from the rest of the population. We lived there for almost a year. My mother came around, but she said she couldn't deal with us because she was being evicted. Looking back, I realize she had a major drug problem. I don't know what she was using then in the '70s, but she eventually graduated to crack. On Christmas Eve, December 24, 1975, her parental rights were terminated, and we were officially made wards of the state.

But we had nowhere to go. At that point we still couldn't be put into regular foster care with other children because of the hepatitis. That's when Baptist Children's Services stepped up and said, "We'll care for them. We'll find a house." One of the nurses who had been caring for us at the hospital, a Miss Ford, offered to go along and serve as housemother. So all seven of us, plus Miss Ford, moved into the house at 3700 Spring Garden Street.

The situation wasn't exactly ideal. Miss Ford was a God-fearing woman, but she didn't take no mess. She was verbally and physically abusive. There were times she would line us up in size order, take the biggest spatula she could find, and whip everybody. If you peed your pants, you got whipped. If you didn't do well in school, you got whipped. My sister Candace told me that one day in school, her teacher had asked the children, "Name one person you would not want to be like and explain why." There were two brothers living in the house behind ours, and they could see and hear everything that went on. One of them answered, "I wouldn't want to be Candace because I can hear her being beat every night."

Fortunately, besides Miss Ford, we had a house-keeper named Miss McCall who was a good, kind woman. Eventually Miss Ford left, and Miss McCall took her place. Things got better then. But maybe it was too late for the older kids, I don't know. Because they just began disappearing. It began when Tyra was 16 or 17. She went off to school one day and just never came back. After that Rodney followed, just up and left. Then Crystal took off. We found out later they'd gone to live with members of our mother's family.

I went off to Charles Drew Elementary School. That school was incredible. They had a Black male principal and five or six Black male teachers. They ran a tight ship, man. You knew who was in charge. It was at Charles Drew that I ran into the first person I now think of as a guide in my life. See, it's my theory that throughout life there are people sent to help you along, to guide you to the next place you're supposed to be. And my first guide was Frank Witherspoon, the science teacher who was in charge of the school safety patrol. I saw these guys walking around school wearing their orange belts. They were like the police in school, and I thought "Whoa! That is what I want!" I went to Mr. Witherspoon and said, "How can I be a safety?" He laughed and said, "Andre, you aren't but in fourth grade. You have to wait at least a year." So I waited, and Mr. Witherspoon kept an eye on me, and next year I became a safety. That was something. We had badges that said "sergeant" and "lieutenant" and even "captain"! I could not have been prouder.

Being on the safety patrol made a huge difference in my life. It kept my behavior circumscribed. I knew that guys on the patrol were supposed to set an example. You couldn't be failing and be a safety. You couldn't have bad manners. As the next few years went by, I kept moving up the ranks on the patrol, eventually being named its "Commander in Chief." Things might not have been the greatest at home, but through his support, Mr. Witherspoon exposed me to a different reality. At school, it didn't matter that I didn't have a mother or a father. It didn't matter that sometimes I looked through the phonebook, calling anybody listed as "N. Coleman" to ask "Are you my mom?" Because when I came to school, I was somebody.

I grabbed other opportunities that school provided. In seventh grade I was recruited to be part of a gifted program that was run out of Drexel University. They gave us student IDs, and we had access to the university's library and gym and other facilities. We actually took some classes there. It was incredible. That ID they gave us—it was like a gold card. With that card, I didn't have to run the streets. On Saturdays, I could take my card and go play pickup basketball at Drexel all day long. When I had homework to do, I didn't have to go to the public library, which was a place you could get beat up. Just like Mr. Witherspoon had connected me to a different reality than the one I lived in, that program connected me to another world. Other good things happened. I became active at the West Philadelphia Community Center. A lady there I knew as Miss Barbara nominated me as Young Man of the Year. We went to a banquet on a chartered bus. I wore a suit and tie. It was beautiful.

So I consider Mr. Witherspoon, Miss Barbara, and the people at the Drexel program all guides at that point in my life. And you know what? I think of somebody else who was a guide in a completely different way. Our housemother, Miss McCall, had a sister, Miss Irene.

Andre Coleman

That woman was the meanest, nastiest lady I ever met. She'd slap and beat me for no reason. One time, and I swear this is true, she said, "I'm sorry, Andre; I'm not going to beat you no more." I said, "But that's what you said last time." And that made her so mad she beat me again! Anyway, as I dealt with Miss Irene, I thought, "I don't care what this lady thinks about me. I'm gonna be better than her. I'm gonna let her behavior motivate me. Right now she's an adult and I'm a child and I can't do much. But I'm going to be an adult someday, and we'll see who comes out ahead." She wanted to push me down, keep me down. But in my mind I said, "No, ma'am. You have no idea, but you're doing me a favor. You're just making me stronger."

This kind of pattern went on. Positive things kept happening; guides kept appearing in my life. But this is the important thing to remember about guides: They can take you to the next stage in your life. But you have to choose to step on the ship in order to be transported. If you don't reach out and take that helping hand, it can't do you any good. A time was coming when I almost forgot that lesson myself.

My home life continued to be up and down. Miss McCall did her best. But things happened. Another group of brothers and sisters moved in with us, and they were terrible, just terrible. They fought each other; they tried to fight us. I thought, "Dang, these people are gonna drag me down. I gotta stay clear of them." Then, when I was 13, our caseworkers called us together and said, "Your mother has got herself together. She has a house. Do you want to go live with her?"

Over the years we'd seen our mother from time to time. She was in North Philly. During our visits to her, I thought, "This ain't great. She's living around some rough people." So when they asked if we wanted to go live with her, I said, "I'm staying right here, Jack." But my older brother Edward said, "That's my mom, and I'm going with her." And he left. For a couple of weeks things seemed OK. He kept coming to school, he was clean, he was saying, "Oh, it's great." Then he stopped coming to school, and then we lost touch with him entirely for three, four years. Eventually we learned that he'd gone home one day and found a padlock on the door. She'd left him, gotten back on drugs and taken off. He was fifteen years old. He managed to follow her to New Jersey, like an abandoned puppy. When Miss McCall heard about this, she said, "Tell Eddie he can always come back to us." But he was proud and embarrassed and he wouldn't come back. He's been drifting ever since. I work in a prison; he's *been* in prison.

Andre Coleman

I started high school at Creative and Performing Arts, majoring in theater. Then one of those crazy things happened that happen when you're in the foster system. My caseworker told me, "You're going to take a trip this weekend. We're going to Thornbury. It's another group home, but you're just going to spend a weekend there now and then." I packed a few things, and we drove miles through the countryside to this house where she dropped me off. And the weekend passed, and no one came for me, and time went on and on, and finally the caseworker said, "Oh, you're going to stay here." And that was it. I never got to say goodbye to my friends, my sisters, Miss McCall.

At Thornbury, the houseparents were a young white couple who didn't know anything about Black boys. The residents were all Black guys, older than me, who had some serious emotional and psychological issues. A little while after I got there, I saw one of them punch a hole in the stove. He broke his hand; they sent him to the psych ward.

It was a bad, bad time in my life. I rebelled. I was like, "I've been trying so hard to stay positive, and I get this?" I was in a crazy environment, and I went crazy too. We basically did whatever we wanted. We threatened the staff. One guy stole the houseparents' car and wrecked it. We skipped school for weeks at a time. I was miserable and angry. The only bright spot was Rob, a part-time worker at the house. He was a Black guy who played basketball with me and talked with me about books and movies. I didn't recognize him at the time, but he was another guide. Even at my worst, he saw I had potential and hung in there with me. I came home from school one day and went looking for my man Kevin, the guy in the house I hung with the most. But Kevin was gone. He'd been kicked out of the house and sent to the Youth Emergency Shelter, which I knew was hell on earth. At the shelter, there was no pretense of a home environment; you'd be fighting every day to keep people from stealing your sneakers. I was furious and mouthing off when one of the adults said, "You know who else was supposed to be shipped off to the shelter? You. And if it wasn't for Rob standing up for you, saying you could be somebody, you'd be gone now too."

That was instrumental. That blew me away. I never knew what kind of danger I'd been in. And this man who, believe me, I had not been all that nice to, had stood up for me and said, "Andre can make it. Don't do him like that." I owe Rob more than I can ever repay. If I'd been sent to that shelter—I don't even want to think about what I would have become.

Not long after that, the white houseparents left and a Black woman and her adult sons moved in as houseparents. They were Mama Hector and her boys Joe and John, who were around 23, 24 years old. And things began to turn around again. I began looking around me for positive opportunities instead of rebelling against the things I couldn't change. I got a job at Arby's, and before long I was an assistant manager with keys to the store. I was making money and going to school and making As and Bs instead of the Cs and Ds I'd been pulling. It was like my mind was waking up. I thought, "I remember this! I remember success! I remember excelling! This is how things are supposed to be!" By the time I graduated high school, I'd turned things around so completely that when my high school created the Frederick Douglass Award, the school's award to the outstanding African American senior, I was its first recipient. I remember the assistant principal there, Dr. Grassty—another guide—talking to me during my senior year. He knew my situation; he knew things hadn't always been good for me. He encouraged me to drop by his office any time to talk. I'd go there and complain about stuff going on at the house and he'd say, "Andre, that's only where you lay your head at night. Just look at it like that. You can come to school and leave all that behind. Here, you can be anything you want to be."

I've thought about Dr. Grassty's words many times in the years that followed. I've thought about how I can pass on what he and all those other guides have taught me. Today I'm a correctional officer at Chester County Prison in Pennsylvania. My early days on the job were rocky. A lot of guys who do that job—they have serious personal issues. They do things on the job that shouldn't be done. I came in and spoke out against the abusive practices that I saw, and a lot of people turned against me as a snitch. But I defied them with every inch of my being. I decided when I took that job, I was going to dispel every stereotype of the bad correctional officer. And things on the job have gotten better, a whole lot better. A lot more officers are on board about wanting to do things the right way, the decent, humane way. I like to think I've had a hand in making that happen.

Part of the reason that I am comfortable working in a prison today is that in a sense, I grew up in a jail. I couldn't go home, not to the home that was really mine. A lot of decisions were made for me that I didn't have any input in. In that sense, I can relate to inmates' situations. I grew up in a situation that was certainly not the one I would have chosen. But I haven't let that experience determine the man that I've become. I try to show by my example that it's possible to change your environment, rather than let your environment change you.

Ray Jones

About Ray Jones

The son of a career military man, Ray Jones spent his early years moving from one East Coast city to another. But when his father left the family, ten-year-old Ray and his mother and siblings settled in Philadelphia.

As a senior journalism major at Temple University, Ray landed an internship in the office of Philadelphia mayor Wilson Goode. There he became interested in the work of community activists. After college he joined the staff of Chaka Fattah, then a state senator and now a member of Congress. Ray spent ten years working for Rep. Fattah, including a year in Washington. D.C. After returning home to Philadelphia, Ray co-founded Black Men United for Progress, a group dedicated to working with troubled young project residents. He later helped develop Men United for a Better Philadelphia, a group focused on reducing violence in the city.

Community activism is Ray's life. "My calling is to show young Black men that they have positive options," says Ray. "I'm from the same streets that these cats are from. I know how important it is to feel you've got somebody pulling for you. My son, above all, is the force that drives me. He's only 3 now, but I know soon he's going to look to me in order to learn how to be a man. I could not love my daughter more. But in the Black community today, being a good father to a son is a special mission."

Ray and his wife Rhashidah are the parents of two children, Raymond III ("Trey") and Hasina.

Ray Jones Speaks

African American men don't value being fathers. Caring African American fathers do not exist. Black fatherhood happens by accident. Being a Black father is a role you spend your life regretting or denying. We Black men just make babies, we don't take care of them. Black children are rarely planned—they just happen.

Right?

Wrong.

My love for my son has challenged those misconceptions of African American fatherhood. For me, the sacrifice, discipline, planning and hard work that go into being a good father are the same elements that create a great man. As a first-time father at age 41, my first promise to my son was that I would always be there for him. My second promise was that I would provide him with a positive male example. Finally, I promised my son that I would leave a legacy as a father, son, husband, friend and activist for him to use as a guide as he makes his own way in the world. Isn't that what other cultures provide for their sons? Those three promises are very important to me to this day because when I was a young boy growing up, my own father was largely absent.

I am convinced that every man's journey to knowing himself and realizing his potential begins with coming to terms with the first man in his life: his father. Throughout that journey, both the father and the son need to face a number of questions. For example, is there a strong connection or friendship? Or was the relationship one of trauma and disappointment? If it was a painful relationship, how do you move forward? These questions lead to personal growth, and for many it begins the necessary process of healing.

My relationship with my father was damaged early on. My parents were teenage sweethearts. When I was born, my father was 19 and my mother was 18. These teenagers were barely old enough to take care of themselves. And yet when I was born in 1963, they were expected to magically become mature adults and parents. After my birth, my father enlisted in the navy. He spent the next 35 years there and, unfortunately for me, my mom, sister and brother, Uncle Sam kept him away from his family.

Soon after my father's military career began, his marriage to my mother ended. It was the early 1970s, and we lived in the tough Strawberry Mansion neighborhood in North Philadelphia. My mom worked part-time. My father, though legally separated from my mom, wasn't sending any money to help with a growing family. Neighborhood gangs were a major fact of life. Young men in my neighborhood either ran with a gang as a member or ran from a gang as a potential victim. We didn't have too many other choices. The gangs gave us a sense of belonging, and boys who were involved in gang life received special attention from the "cool" people in the neighborhood as well as, in many cases, the cutest girls. At that time I was too young to join the major gangs in the neighborhood. The gangs usually started recruiting boys in their early teens. Instead, I belonged to an elementary school gang—a junior version of a street gang in the neighborhood that we copied and looked up to. We focused on vandalism and recess fights with other boys to deal with the frustration that many of us were experiencing at home and in the neighborhood. Gang life taught us about manhood, in a sense. It taught us to protect and stand up for ourselves. If our families could not provide male role models as guides for a better life, gang leaders stepped in to fill that void.

But gang leaders weren't our only role models. If you were good with your fists or at sports, there were older men who would provide you with advice and show genuine concern for you. In a lot of ways, they would see themselves in you and act as your "old head." An old head was an older male who was respected because he had a reputation for protecting himself well or he was good at sports or attracting girls. Like other young boys looking for direction and attention, I was proud to do whatever I could to be noticed by an old head. Old heads offered an alternative "street example" of a father figure. Often these men would give us advice about girls, maybe even give us some money. The absence of fathers in the neighborhoods allowed some men with questionable character and background to have influence over younger boys. Some of the old heads were working men with wives and children, but others were ex-convicts and street hustlers.

The old head that had the most impact on me was our next-door neighbor, Mr. Blocker. I was torn between wanting to grow up to be a gangster or a family man like him. I used to pretend that Mr. Blocker was my dad. Mr. Blocker was a car mechanic with a good work ethic. When he wasn't repairing cars, he was often dispensing wisdom and kind words to children in the neighborhood. He was the first example I can remember of a positive man taking care of his family. I thought Mr. Blocker must be a very special man because he was there with his family, unlike my own father. Not only did he take care of his own children, but he made us other neighborhood kids feel that we were important, too. He would tell us if we were doing something wrong, and encourage us if he noticed us demonstrating a skill. Although I looked up to the gang leaders in the neighborhood, I recognized in Mr. Blocker what I really yearned for: a committed father. Mr. Blocker's existence helped me cope with the absence of my own father. He never seemed to get tired of answering questions about cars. He always had a smile and a greeting for all the kids and neighbors. I often thought that the perfect father would be a combination of a family man like Mr. Blocker and a street-smart old head. Both of those examples were in my neighborhood. I think I benefited from seeing both of those types of men on the block, but what I really wanted was a relationship with my own father.

In the meantime, Raymond Thomas Jones, Senior

had become like a ghost. My dad was someone I would overhear my mother talking and cursing about to our relatives. After a while, I couldn't remember what he was like at all. I used to pretend that he was trying to get our family back together, but that his job in the Navy prevented him from coming to North Philadelphia. But questions kept haunting me: Does he know how dangerous it is where we live? Why doesn't he at least check on us?

As I reached my teen years, I was filled with a tremendous amount of anger about the disconnect with my father. I also resented my mother's authority. I told myself I was becoming a man. She couldn't teach me how to be a man, I reasoned, so why should I listen to her? I developed a temper, which led to fights with neighborhood kids. I wouldn't let anyone know if my feelings were hurt. If I thought someone was trying to bully me or make me feel bad, I would be the first to put his hands up to fight. I was floundering emotionally with no real direction.

Finally some friends of mine left a small package of marijuana joints at my house. I was trying to sell them to another kid when my mother caught me. I think my mom saw a future of crime and jail time in front of me, so she called my father.

In response, my father called me. This was the first time I could remember him calling because he was concerned about me. I didn't respond well. I thought he was a little late calling to give me the "I am your father; what are you doing with your life?" lecture. But the calls kept coming, and sometimes I called him as well. We both struggled through this period. We yelled most of the time, trying to communicate, but usually our talks ended in frustration and disappointment. My anger was deep, and I think my father felt bad because he had never been there for me.

After a while, though, our relationship began to slowly change for the better. I believe the turning point was a phone call I placed to him when I was 18. I called my father and spoke to him from my heart. I told him about it all—my frustration, my anger, and my rage. After I was through speaking, I let him speak, uninterrupted. I began to really listen to him—not just hear the words coming from the end of the phone. That was our real beginning.

My father told me about his experience of being a teenage father. He told me how scared he had been when I was born, and how little he had known about being a man, a husband, or a father. My grandfather, he explained, had not showed him any affection as a child; neither had my grandfather prepared him for the responsibilities and sacrifice a father makes to keep a family together. So, in a sense, he failed us because he had been failed. He was quick to tell me that his explanation was not the same as an excuse. He told me that he could have done better as a father and a man and did not. He apologized to me, and that helped me a lot. For a long time, I think I felt I was not worthy of having a father. He set me straight about that, making it clear that it was he who had failed in our relationship, not me. I began to feel a lot better about myself and my own future.

My father's description of his own childhood was an eye-opener. When you are a child, you think that your parents are bigger than life. They can do anything; they have no problems; they have all the answers, right? But finally I began to see my father as just a man. He was a man who made mistakes, a man who had faults; but he was a man who was reaching out and trying to become a better father, even at this late stage.

Getting to know my father, not as some fantasy figure but as a flawed human being, was at times a painful process. But I'm convinced that acknowledging the pain and insecurities that are part of life are a necessary part of growing up. Maybe that is especially difficult for young African American men. Like many of my friends, I had worked hard on my "cool pose" exterior—that false front of bravado that says, "You can't hurt me" or "I don't care." Often that front masks a deep hurt and a longing that too many of us carry into adulthood. Growing up without a father makes it especially hard for us to admit our hurts and vulnerabilities. As a kid, being the oldest male child, I felt responsible for protecting myself as well as my sister, brother and mother. I remember wondering who in the world was going to protect me. I became a substitute father figure at a very young age, often encouraged by my mother. Looking back, I think life was just as difficult for my mother, who was raising three kids without a man to help provide for the children and protect her. The absence of a father affects everyone— including the missing father. A part of me has had to forgive my mother and myself for having the unrealistic expectation that a boy should act like a man.

When I reached my early twenties, my father and I began what would ultimately turn out to be a ten-year odyssey in discovering each other as men. We were both past the stage where we expected to have a typical father-son relationship. We accepted that we would start where we were—using the past as a beginning and realizing that the "end" of our relationship had not been written. We are very good friends now. We accept each other for who we are and have come to terms with the past. That does not mean that I do not wish things had been different. I often think, "What decisions would I have made differently if my father had been there to teach me how to be a man? Would I have excelled in school, instead of struggling? Would I have had a healthier view of relationships with women?" But instead of being embittered, I use my experiences with my father to help me raise my own son, Trey. My father advises me, "Make new mistakes with your kids. Learn from my mistakes, and don't do the same things!" Those are wise words, and I try hard to take advantage of that advice. Coming to term with my father's absence has made me, in my view, a better father and a better father figure to the young men that I come into contact with.

Today, I am a co-founder of the group Men United For A Better Philadelphia. I try to reach young men on the street corners and provide them with alternatives to the lives that they are currently living. Doing my work, I'm back on the same streets I grew up on. I look at those boys now and I see myself. Through social service information, job development programs, and direct action such as protests and boycotts, we extend ourselves to men and young boys to help them help themselves. We Men United are doing our best to display the full character of African American men. Many of us are fathers, and we are making our presence known as leaders in the neighborhood, protecting and providing for communities on the margins. I am the "old head" now. I want to protect and nurture young men and boys because I see the bigger picture: how the cycle of abandonment leads to dysfunction and self-destructive behavior that can last a lifetime. I have learned that when you feel as if you are not worthy of affection and love, often from a father, you act out in protest. You can hurt others, and you can also hurt yourself. I know how that feels because I have lived that experience.

What is the value of living up to responsibility as an African American father? Mr. Blocker's example showed me that being a responsible African American father has value in and of itself, period. In a neighborhood where expectations of Black men were low, he set the standard higher. In doing so, he provided an example of manhood that helped me see the possibilities within myself.

I am now, in many ways, my father. Although I am

present for my own child, I make mistakes that Trey, my son, will someday talk with me about—probably in a loud voice. I have expectations of my son that he may grow up to accept or reject. I will leave a legacy of life-lessons, experiences, mistakes and achievements that will fall somewhere between my high hopes for it and what value it will actually have for my son.

Discovering that my father was and is just a man continues to help me as I mature. In his turn, Trey will discover that although I am his father, I, too, am just a flawed human being. When fathers and sons can reach out, acknowledging our need for one another, all our futures become brighter.

Calvin Sims

About Calvin Sims

Calvin Sims, a computer consultant earning a six-figure income, was riding in a chauffeur-driven limousine on his way to speak to an international banking conference in Zurich, Switzerland. He was thinking how strange it was that he, an unwanted poor boy from the slums of Atlanta with a ninth-grade education, should have arrived at this place in his life. A thought occurred to him: "When you talk to people and tell them what they are capable of, they will believe you. You are the proof."

Upon returning home, Calvin dedicated himself to reaching young men and women who society had said were unreachable. He founded StoryTellers of the American Frontier, a non-profit organization designed to use storytelling—especially the stories of the American cowboy and cowgirl—to inspire young people. These days, Calvin spends more of his time on horseback than riding in limos. Dressed in full cowboy gear, he visits schools to talk about old-fashioned values like integrity, character, and respect for education. At Calvin's Teaching Farm in Newborn, Georgia, groups of young people from schools, the juvenile justice system, churches, and other organizations gather to participate in inspirational programs and eat great food cooked over an open fire. Calvin is the author of six children's books. His most recent, *Lawman: The Bass Reeves Story*, tells of a man born a slave in Texas who grew to be regarded as "the greatest lawman in the West."

Calvin and his wife Diana are the proud parents of seven children and grandparents of nine.

Calvin Sims Speaks

My childhood ended very early. When my mother went to work, she would often leave me in the care of her best friend, a wonderful woman I came to know as Momma. One day while at work, my mother took sick. She was rushed to the hospital, where she died. I think she probably had a brain tumor. I was four years old.

No one from my family ever came to get me. I had four brothers, all of whom were at least twelve years older than me. My mother had been married twice. She bore two sons with each husband. As I've put the scattered pieces of the story together, I have figured out her marriage to husband number two was in trouble and they were separated when she conceived me. I was not her husband's child.

Calvin Sims

My biological father disappeared, and my mother's family turned their backs on me. I never left Momma's home until I was 16. Soon after leaving, I joined the Marines. It was during the Vietnam War, but I was convinced that my chances of survival in Vietnam were better than they were in Vine City Bottom. Vine City was the most violent, poverty-stricken neighborhood in Atlanta during the late '60s and early '70s. It was so bad there that I looked up to and envied the people who lived in the projects. At least there, there was some effort at maintenance—when a window got broken, it was eventually replaced. But we were so poor that in the summer, we simply stopped paying our gas bill and let the gas be turned off. I don't remember a weekend that there wasn't gunfire in the neighborhood.

Right after my mother's death, my life seemed pretty good. Though I had no contact with my biological family, my new foster family was sympathetic to the toddler who had lost his mother. I was showered with toys and affection. My fifth birthday was like something out of a fairy tale. The *Davy Crockett* TV show was all the rage, and I got everything from the coonskin cap to a toy version of "Betsy," Davy's trusty rifle that had killed many a "bar."

I have no memory of feeling grief at my mother's

passing. Perhaps I did not understand, or perhaps I was distracted by my new-found fortune. My pleasant life lasted less than a year, or until one of my foster siblings had a child of his own. Gradually, I became the stepchild, the unwanted little orphan. I remember one of my foster siblings asking me if I knew what a "bastard" was. I had no idea. Apparently, everyone was in on the humiliating secret except me. I did not know what a bastard was, but even at the age of 6, I came to realize that I was one and that it was not a good thing.

I became obsessed with finding out what a bastard was and what it had to do with me. The definitions I read in dictionaries were confusing. The whole concept did not make sense. From what I read, it seemed that the blame for adult behavior rested on the shoulders of the child, while the misdeeds of the parents who conceived that child were not addressed. Words like "illegitimate," "bastard," and "born out of wedlock" all referred to the child, who was innocent. Where were the words that described the adults who had created that child?

Soon, my life became one long string of humiliations. No one felt sorry for me any more. I seemed to be in the way. While my foster mother was almost always away working, my so-called siblings missed no opportunity to let me know that I was not a part of their family. Their children were royalty, and I was a peasant. I became the target of physical and psychological abuse. By the age of 8, I was being molested by each of my four foster siblings, all of whom were in their 20s.

My reaction was one that I would later learn is common. I kept quiet, accepting the abuse as a fact of my life. Perhaps the most awful thing about child abuse is the way abused, neglected and/or molested children react to this cruelty. Most children internalize their mistreatment and blame themselves. They believe it is their fate to suffer in silence. If they object, they think, they will only expose their shame to the world.

I moved through life in a haze of confusion until I reached third grade and found myself a student of the dreaded "Mrs. Moore," said to be the meanest teacher in the school. Little did I know that I would sing Mrs. Moore's praises for the rest of my life.

Mrs. Moore noticed me. She saw a sad little boy who loved school, but seemed to never want to go home. She decided to do something that would change my life. She gave me a book, *Ivanhoe*. It was an exciting novel about heroic characters who risked everything in order to do right, defend the weak, and prove themselves worthy of love. I devoured *Ivanhoe*. Mrs. Moore told me that if I was ever unhappy with the world around me, I could escape into a good book. Through books, I could leave Vine City and meet kings and queens and scientists and warriors. I could not only travel the universe; I could even travel through time.

I discovered through books that there was a vast world out there that was different from the world I lived in. I learned there were people who were different from the people that I lived with.

I learned about character and integrity. I learned about honor and loyalty and faith. I learned that an individual could affect the world around him. I learned about men who drew together not to prey on the weak, but to live by a code of honor. They were men like Atticus Finch, the father in another of my favorite books, *To Kill a Mockingbird*. Atticus Finch, a mild-mannered attorney who defended a wrongfully accused man, became my ideal of a good man, as well as a good father. I saw that his son, Jem, was going to grow up to be as good a man. Although Jem's little sister, Scout, pestered him like a plague of locusts, he loved and protected her. Everywhere I looked in my world, I saw the opposite of men like Atticus Finch. I saw men who lived to exploit the weak. They rejected their responsibilities. They profited from the misfortunes of others. They seemed weak and cowardly to me. As my values grew more different from the ones I saw around me, I found life even more difficult.

Naturally, the young people growing up in that environment absorbed what they observed around them. Like most small children, I was bullied constantly and forced to hand over my lunch money on a regular basis. But one day, that all changed.

As I was walking to school, the lead bully in the neighborhood approached me. He was probably 12. As usual, he stuck out his hand for me to place my quarter in his palm. But when I reached into my pocket, I found only lint. During that moment, I remember seeing two distinct visions. First, I saw my quarter lying on the kitchen table where it was placed each morning and where I had left it. Then, I saw my life flash before my eyes. I knew that I was about to die.

I had read in one of my books that when you are up against impossible odds and about to be attacked, the only thing to do is hurl yourself headfirst into battle. I decided that since I was about to be beaten, I would strike the first blow. I had never been in a fight, but I had seen plenty. I did what I saw others do. The bigger boy was confidently facing away from me talking to his fellow bullies when I caught him with my fist right under his jaw. His jaw broke.

As he lay on the ground, writhing in pain, his startled friends announced that they were going to kill me. I was like a deer caught in the headlights, too frightened to run. Suddenly, the older men—the winos, who were standing on the same corner—intervened. They were slapping each other on the back and hooting and hollering about what I had done. They started calling me "Joe Louis" after the famous Black boxer. They informed the other bullies that they would have to answer to them if any one of them touched me. They assured me that if anyone ever bothered me, to just let them know.

From that moment on, I had nothing to fear on my way to school. In that way, my life was better. But I still lived in that house. The abuse at home continued. I would do whatever I was told, then find somewhere to hide with a book. I would read to keep from seeing the world I lived in. When I watched TV as well, I would see normal families where the children were loved and protected by both father and mother. In Vine City, even having two parents was a rarity.

Relatively safe on the street now, I began to explore the world beyond my front yard. I befriended many of the boys who had tormented me. Because I had defeated an older boy, I became something of a leader. This made me feel wonderful. Now I had people who actually looked up to me, who listened to what I had to say as if it were important. I had discovered what is perhaps the most addictive substance on Earth: Acceptance.

We boys formed a strong bond that was more powerful than a family. I don't know what the other boys were going through at home. We didn't talk about it, but somehow we knew that we were all going through something. Something that wasn't right. We were living in a sick society and struggling to survive.

Together we felt strong, almost invincible. We started to steal things. We became more aggressive. I went from being bullied to being a bully. Our numbers grew as young boys our age opted to join us rather than to oppose us. Before long, we caught the attention of certain adults in the neighborhood—the real gangsters.

While we were shoplifting, these men were robbing, burglarizing, running prostitutes, dealing drugs, and stealing cars. These were the closest things we had to heroes in our world. We mimicked them and emulated them as best we could. We tried to dress, walk, and talk like them.

I, however, had a dilemma. I did not really want to be like these men. Alone with my books and my thoughts, I still idealized a very different kind of man. Nor did I really want to do any of the things that we did—the stealing, the break-ins, the bullying. I felt trapped. I hated what I was becoming, but I had found a group of people who accepted me.

I really wanted to go to school and get an education and get out of there. I thought if I got out of Vine City, I might be able to work in a factory. When I was really flying high, I dreamed about becoming a teacher, but that was such a lofty goal I quickly dismissed it. It was as if I said I was going to become President. For the most part, though, I did not think of education as a means to a particular job or income. I just hungered for the knowledge it would give me. Even as a youngster, I had realized that knowledge gave me power. Because reading had given me an enormous vocabulary, I could slyly insult people, make fun of them, without them knowing I was doing it.

The other boys didn't know I read in private. I could be kicked out of the gang if they knew that I spent much of my time reading. I had to sneak away to go to the library. Everyone just laughed at the way I talked and the "big ole words" I used sometimes.

Calvin Sims

But finally my language got me a different kind of attention. A particular man approached me. He was the top gangster in the neighborhood. He was like the Mayor of Vine City. Nobody would dare pull any criminal activity in the area without going through him first. He said that he had heard that I was smart and that I knew Shakespeare. I was nervous and not sure how to answer him, but I admitted that I had read some Shakespeare.

Some of the men standing around began to laugh scornfully. "Who??" they said. He shot them a glance, and they were quiet. He asked me if I knew any of Shakespeare's work by heart, so I began reciting Hamlet's famous speech, the one that begins:

"To be, or not to be? That is the question.

Whether 'tis nobler in the mind to suffer

 the slings and arrows of outrageous fortune,

Or to take arms against a sea of troubles

and, by opposing, end them . . ."

When I stopped, he started laughing; so did everyone else. But this time they were not laughing at me. They were laughing in a kind of disbelief, but in admiration, because they had never seen anything like that, not around there.

I began to spend a lot of time with this guy. I was

like his little mascot. He took me out and bought me sharp clothes. He had me carry his rolls of cash and his handgun. My job was to stay near him so he could get his gun and money when he needed them, but so he'd be clean if the cops searched him. I was nine years old.

My foster siblings knew what it meant that I had become sidekick to this man. If the word got out what they had been doing to me, they would literally disappear. The molestation and abuse stopped suddenly and completely. They still did little if anything to help me, but at least no one ever touched me again.

Now, I could go to school in the open. It was accepted in the neighborhood that I was a young man who had a lot of book smarts as well as street smarts. The gang leader had made it clear that the best gangster had both. He also made it clear that no one was to touch a hair on my head.

I had achieved a status where I no longer had to be a bully. But I still found myself doing things that really made me feel bad, just to fit in. While I no longer had to worry about being assaulted, I was still addicted to acceptance. If I couldn't come up with some excuse, I continued to go along with the crowd when they did some criminal activity. Later, when I was alone, I was tormented by what I had done.

Calvin Sims

Each time, right before I did something that I would later regret, I felt as though I was standing at a fork in the road. Each tine in the fork represented a path that I could take. When I chose to do the thing that I would later regret, I was choosing the path that led to acceptance. That path became harder and harder for me to take as I matured and learned to think for myself.

Doing things opposed to my own values in order to be accepted by the crowd was so contrary to the way I imagined my heroes would behave. Such behavior seemed weak and worthless when I thought about men like World War II Commander Dwight David Eisenhower, who later became president, or frontier lawmen like Wyatt Earp and Bass Reeves. Even the simple TV characters like Ward Cleaver on *Leave It to Beaver* or Dr. Stone on *Father Knows Best* were like giants to me. These men provided for their families and supported them. They didn't base their actions on being accepted by others. They were the ones who set examples for others to follow.

Gradually, I began to see that while one path at the fork of the road led to acceptance by others, the other leads to self-acceptance—and, more importantly, to self-respect. I began to understand that self-respect is of supreme importance. Any other form of respect now seems superficial to me. The respect that I had been seeking from others is a cheap and fragile thing. It can be lost in the blink of an eye. Others can snatch it away at any time. Yet self-respect is mine to keep as long as I choose the right path when I stand at a fork in the road.

And what is that right path? It is the path that leads to doing the right thing, the honest thing, the kind thing. It is the path that leads to helping others, rather than thinking only of myself.

Today when I stand at a fork in the road, I no longer look for the path that will lead to acceptance by others. I look for the path that will make me respect myself later, when I am alone with my thoughts. As I choose my path in life, I think of the little boy I was. I try to be the man that little boy needed in his life—the man he could look up to.

Elijah Anderson

About Elijah Anderson

Elijah Anderson was born in the Mississippi Delta during World War II. Like so many rural poor Black Southerners, his parents made their living in the context of racial segregation. As part of the "great migration," the family ventured north to South Bend, Indiana, where Eli's father found work in the foundry of the Studebaker Corporation. In South Bend, Eli attended the local public schools, where he was a precocious reader. Later he joined the Cub Scouts and then the Boy Scouts, organizations that were critical for his later development. At age 10, he sold newspapers on downtown street corners. At 11, he set pins at a downtown bowling alley. At 12, he went door to door to downtown merchants, asking for steady work. Marion Forbes, the owner of a local typewriter company, hired him. At Forbes Typewriter, Eli emptied wastebaskets, washed windows, and did handyman work. Serving in a kind of apprenticeship, he learned to clean and repair typewriters, and worked there until he graduated from high school. Mr. Forbes allowed him time off to engage in school athletics, including basketball, track, and other sports. As many of his athletic peers began to look forward to higher education by way of athletic scholarships, he was inspired by their example and began to look forward to college as well.

After graduating high school, Eli began classes at the Indiana University extension in South Bend. He did so well that he earned a scholarship to enroll at the main I.U. campus in Bloomington, Indiana, where he fell in love with books and academic work. He graduated from I.U. with a bachelor's degree and then went on to the University of Chicago for his master's degree and Northwestern University for his Ph.D. From there, he was recruited and appointed Assistant Professor at Swarthmore College, and later recruited by the University of Pennsylvania, where he rose from assistant professor to associate professor to professor, and then to an endowed professorship and ultimately to a distinguished professorship, with a secondary appointment in the Wharton School. After teaching at Penn for many years, he has recently joined the faculty of Yale University as the William K. Lanman, Jr. Professor of Sociology. He has written a number of books considered classics of sociology, all focusing on race and inequality in the United States.

Elijah Anderson

Elijah Anderson Speaks

When you think of a scientist, you probably imagine someone in a white coat, mixing chemicals in a test tube. I am a scientist, but not that kind. I don't work with test tubes and Bunsen burners. I am a social scientist—someone who studies human society and the way people within that society relate to one another. My special field of study is urban ethnography. At Yale University, where I am a professor, I teach courses in topics like "Urban Sociology" (the study of cities) and "Ethnography of the African American Community" (ethnography is about describing and documenting a current culture—in this case, modern African American culture.)

But like those scientists in white coats, I have my own laboratory: the social settings of the city. These are the places I study in order to do my research. For instance, my first book was called *A Place on the Corner*. In order to write it, I spent three years on the south side of Chicago, hanging out and engaging in "participant-observation" at a bar and liquor store on what I called "Jelly's corner." There I interviewed and listened to the men who were regulars there, learning all about their small community and how it worked.

I paid special attention to how those men constantly established and re-established their status in everyday life. I wrote copious field notes about my research experiences, and those notes formed the basis for my book.

More recently, I have written a book called *Code of the Street: Decency, Violence, and the Moral Life of the Inner City*. I based it on research and observations done in the city of Philadelphia. In the book, I focus on Germantown Avenue, a major artery that runs through the city. It begins in some very well-to-do "suburbs" within the city, then moves into more middle-class neighborhoods, and eventually into the heart of inner-city Philadelphia. For the purposes of *Code of the Street*, Germantown Avenue became my laboratory.

Let me give you a look at Germantown Avenue, and tell you about some of my observations there.

The top of the avenue lies in the affluent community called Chestnut Hill. It is a mostly white area, although becoming more racially mixed. The houses are generally large, surrounded by lawns and trees. The shopping district is full of small, upscale businesses: gourmet food shops, a camera shop, jewelry stores, clothing boutiques. A casual, taken-for-granted mixing of the races is common. You see integrated groups of children on the playground. At the bank, there is cheerful interaction between Black and white tellers and clients. Mixed-race groups of friends stroll past the shops. Everyone is polite and seems relaxed. When people pass one another on the sidewalk, they often make eye contact and smile. Folks stand chatting quietly on the sidewalk, sometimes with their backs to the street. You don't get the feeling that there is any hostility or that people are on guard against being hassled or insulted or robbed. There is a pleasant, civil atmosphere.

Down the hill, Germantown Avenue wanders through the communities of Mount Airy, Germantown, Nicetown, and then reaches Broad Street in North Philadelphia. As the Avenue moves south, the scene changes rapidly. The racial mix changes to become more evenly mixed, then almost completely Black, working-class, and poor. The large, affluent homes of Chestnut Hill disappear, replaced first by tidy single-family homes and then by row homes, boarded-up buildings, and vacant lots. Boutiques and trendy restaurants vanish, giving way to pawn shops, barbeque joints, liquor stores, and storefront churches. There are bars on windows and riot gates outside of businesses.

Along with the visual differences, there is a very noticeable change in atmosphere. By the time the avenue reaches the Broad Street area, it is striking how closely people seem to watch their backs. They are very careful how they present themselves. They keep a close eye on others who are sharing their space. People avoid making eye contact for too long. If they don't, a hostile "What you looking at?" may result. Young people gathering on the street at times pepper their conversation with loud obscenities, as if daring anyone to object. A noisy argument in the park may move into a nearby alley to be settled with a fight, maybe with guns. There is a sense of simmering anger, of violence lurking under the surface.

Why? Why is the atmosphere so different between communities like Chestnut Hill and North Philly? Why do people in one seem friendly and relaxed, while people in the other tend to act suspicious, cold, and hard? Is it a matter of race, or of income? Are white people or well-off people naturally friendlier and more laid-back than Black or poor people?

Clearly, that isn't true. Anyone who has spent time in the Black community or among poor people has experienced the same warmth, love, and friendship that exist in any human community. But in public, behavior is very different. The realities of ghetto life have created a "street culture" that affects everyone living there.

Elijah Anderson

Even children growing up in the most decent homes have to learn to handle themselves on the street. (I do not use the word "decent" as a moral judgment. Local residents typically say "decent" to mean "committed to conventional, mainstream values." "Street" culture, on the other hand, generally opposes those traditional values.)

Code of the Street

Of all the problems facing the poor inner-city Black community, none is more critical than that of interpersonal violence and aggression. Such violence wreaks havoc daily on the lives of community residents. Increasingly, it spills over into downtown and residential middle-class areas like Chestnut Hill. Muggings, burglaries, carjackings, and drug-related shootings, all of which may leave their victims or innocent bystanders dead, are now common enough to concern all urban and many suburban residents.

The roots of such violence lie in the realities of life among the ghetto poor: the lack of jobs that pay a living wage, limited basic public services (such as police response in emergencies, building maintenance, trash pickup, lighting, and other services that middle class neighborhoods take for granted), the stigma of race, the

113

fallout from rampant drug use and drug trafficking, and the resulting lack of hope for the future. Simply living in such an environment places young people at risk of falling victim to aggressive behavior. It is true that there are often forces in the community that can counteract the negative influences. By far the most powerful is a strong, loving, "decent" (as inner-city residents put it) family that is committed to middle-class values. But the despair in the ghetto has given birth to a second culture, the culture of "the street." The norms of the street often directly oppose the norms of mainstream society.

If you are a young man living in the inner city, you may be thinking, "You don't have to tell me what it's like here. This is my home." And I don't doubt you could tell me a great deal about your daily reality. But sometimes it's hard to look objectively at the environment we live in, especially if it is what we've always known. In my opinion, it is extremely useful to recognize the way these two orientations—decent and street—affect you and your community. How the two coexist and interact has important consequences for residents, particularly for youngsters growing up in the inner city.

Above all, this environment means that even young people whose home lives reflect mainstream values have been forced to learn to handle themselves in a street-oriented environment. This is because the street culture has evolved a "code of the street"—a set of informal rules governing public behavior, particularly violence. The rules dictate how people are supposed to behave and how they are to respond if they are challenged. They set rules for the use of violence. The rules have been established and are enforced mainly by street-oriented people. But on the streets, the distinction between "street" and "decent" isn't very relevant. Everybody knows that if the rules are broken, there are penalties. For this reason, even families who are thoroughly "decent"—who generally oppose the values of the street code—reluctantly encourage their children to become familiar with that code. They know their children need the code of the streets in order to negotiate the inner city environment.

At the heart of the code is the issue of respect— loosely defined as being treated "right" or being granted one's "props." Respect is a universal human desire. However, in the troublesome environment of the inner city, what one deserves in the way of respect becomes increasingly problematic and uncertain. A major reason for this uncertainty is residents' feelings about official law enforcement. The police are generally viewed as representing the dominant white society and as unconcerned about inner city residents. When police are called, they may not respond, leading many residents to feel they must take extraordinary measures to defend themselves and their loved ones. Respect for the law erodes, and "street justice" fills the void. In this context, a person's "street cred" becomes his security. But maintaining street credibility takes constant effort. It's never accomplished once and for all. And the attempt to preserve and build it up feeds into an endless cycle of argument, violence, and then payback. Respect or street credibility is both hard-won and easily lost, so it must constantly be guarded. With the right amount, individuals can avoid being bothered in public. This is so very important, for if they are bothered, not only may they face physical danger, but they will have been disgraced or "dissed," thereby losing some of that all-important cred. Many of the forms that dissing can take may seem petty and even bewildering to middle-class people (maintaining eye contact for too long, for example), but for people living in persistent racialized urban poverty, self-esteem is an extremely competitive affair. Young people become profoundly envious of each other, as any positive quality or special possession raises one person's status above another's. Competition for status may be settled through various sorts of contests, including verbal sparring, argument, and, finally, physical violence.

As the above shows, the code of the street is actually a cultural adaptation, a useful way of surviving the harsh realities of the inner city. But living by the code places young people in a sort of "Catch-22," a situation that leads to inevitable defeat. Because while living by the code may be an effective survival mechanism on the street, its open display seriously damages the young man's chances of success in the outer world. Few employers know how to tell the difference between a genuine thug—a criminal—and a decent kid who has adopted the thug dress, speech, look, and behavior to protect himself on the street. The result? In an increasingly competitive unskilled-job market, employers develop more reasons to continue discriminating against young Black men. This discrimination undercuts those young men's economic viability, thereby limiting their choices in life.

There is no question about it: our inner cities are in crisis. The days when almost any able-bodied man could find a job at a living wage are gone. Our economy has shifted away from manufacturing toward service and high technology, areas requiring specialized training. Good jobs are leaving our cities for the suburbs or being shipped overseas to developing countries like India and China. Many of the residents who have the skills and education to leave the inner city have done so, leaving behind the most hopeless and disillusioned.

In order to turn things around in our cities, fundamental changes must be made on all levels, from community to city to state to federal. The first challenge is that the wider "conventional" society and its leaders, especially corporate America, must come to understand the situation for what it is: that centuries of discrimination have led to racialized urban poverty that now places the Black urban poor in untenable circumstances. Building upon such understanding, economic opportunities must be brought back to our cities for young Black men. Gun control must become a reality. We need social programs that will encourage effective mothers, fathers and other role models for our young people, models that will teach personal responsibility at an early age. Our own Black professionals must reach back and encourage young people to take education seriously, and to be able to persuasively point out the rewards of education, both for the individual and the community.

As a social scientist, I am more inclined to report

and analyze what I see than give prescriptions for what I think ought to be. But given a chance to talk to young men who want a better life for themselves, I'd say this: "Take every opportunity to develop what we call 'human capital.' By human capital I mean education, skills, ways of behavior that can serve you outside the 'hood. The fundamental three R's—reading, writing, and 'rithmetic—are absolute necessities for success. Those things become coin: coin that you can trade in order to achieve a better place."

In the ghetto, "street knowledge" and behavior serve as a valuable form of coin. Outside of the ghetto, it is worthless—worse than worthless; it is a barrier to success. Our young men have to "know what time it is," and to be able to "code switch"—to handle themselves on the street, but also be able to adopt conventional behaviors that allow them to succeed in mainstream society. Schooling, standard English, conventional manners—all those are coin of the larger society. They are power. Our young men have shown themselves clever and savvy enough to adopt one set of behaviors to survive in the mean streets of urban America. But if those behaviors are all they know, they are fated to live and, all too often, die in those streets. By adopting another code, our young men have a far better chance of thriving in the world at large. If they learn to practice and to excel by observing the conventions of mainstream behavior, they can negotiate the wider system. And negotiating the system is key to climbing the ladder of success.

Fluke Fluker

About Fluke Fluker

Fluke Fluker is a former Marine sergeant and a basketball player for California State University in Northridge. He has spent twenty-two years coaching basketball at every level from middle school through professional. In 2003, Fluke, now a teacher and coach at Los Angeles' Cleveland High School, joined with fellow teachers Andre Chevalier and Bill Paden to found The Village Nation, a groundbreaking project aimed at closing the achievement gap between African American and white students. The astounding results achieved by the Village Nation have been reported in major media outlets all over the United States. Fluke and his Village Nation co-founders have been featured guests on *Oprah*, where host Oprah Winfrey praised the organization by saying, "The Village Nation serves as a leading example for people who think out of the box." Cleveland High School, the once-failing school that is home to the Village Nation, is now designated as a California Distinguished School. Looking back at the success of the Village Nation, Fluke says, "Our children no longer see themselves as the problem but instead as the solution—they have taken a firm stance in understanding the responsibility that accompanies their culture and heritage."

Fluke Fluker Speaks

I'm not anyone special. I tell kids I meet today, "I was you and you are me." I grew up in the projects of Brooklyn. I hated school! I could barely read, but I got bumped along from grade to grade. I had no vision of any future beyond hanging out and being known.

I can't blame my parents for my attitude. They cared very much. Although my father had just a fifth-grade education, he and my mother both believed in schooling. They prayed and encouraged me. But those seeds of encouragement fell on dry, infertile soil.

I started making the usual stupid choices and hanging with negative people. When I was 17, I got stabbed in a fight. When I woke up, I was handcuffed to a hospital gurney. Trips to court were by now pretty commonplace for me, and I ended up in front of a judge who was, shall we say, acquainted with me. He said, "I do not want to see you again." In the 1970s, that basically meant "Join the military or I'll put you in jail." I chose the military. And given my Billy Badass attitude, I decided to be a Marine.

For me, joining the military was a life-saving experience. I'd always been the guy people would look to and say, "What should we do?" Part of it is my stature—I'm 6 foot 7—and part of it was my God-given athletic ability. I'd been captain of every sports team I'd ever been on. The United States Marines gave me a positive channel for that leadership, a channel that illuminated my natural intelligence and abilities. The Marines gave me the discipline and grounding that I needed for every other aspect of my life. At age 19 and a half, I became the corps's youngest peacetime sergeant.

After my time in the service was over, I wanted to go back to school. My experience in the Marines had given me a taste of success, and I knew now that I could succeed. I was able to get an athletic scholarship to junior college. But at this point I had to face the fact that that my academic skills were weak, extremely weak. I had to take remedial classes—and I mean *really* remedial. Here I was, a USMC sergeant, having to sit there with what were basically *Cat in the Hat* books. It was both humiliating and humbling. My only hope for improvement lay in my acknowledging my strengths and weaknesses and deciding to embrace them both, because I alone owned them. I refused to blame others or to make excuses—these were my issues, and I was going to deal with them. It was later discovered that I have severe dyslexia, a learning disorder which accounted for my difficulties reading. This information was both relieving and enlightening. I was relieved because, finally, I knew the cause of the problem. I was enlightened because I learned about resources and strategies that I could use to compensate for my weaknesses. I had always known I wasn't stupid, so why was reading so hard for me? But dyslexia—to me, that's just like being farsighted or nearsighted. There's no shame in it. Once I was given the tools to overcome dyslexia, I could learn much more easily.

Gradually my abilities improved, and eventually I earned my associate's degree. I also earned a scholarship to California State University, where I completed a bachelor's degree in kinesiology, which is the study of how the body functions and moves. Later I coached at Cal State Northridge while earning my teaching degree.

Glancing back over my life, you can see why I say I was no different from a lot of kids who end up in jail or in the cemetery. To this day, when I see kids being lured by the call of the streets and making negative choices, I see a part of me. And I yearn to reach those kids, to give them a helping hand. My heart aches within me for that child that used to be me. That's why I became a teacher.

I'd attended a rough public school in Brooklyn. But in California I did my student teaching at Beverly

Fluke Fluker

Hills High School—yeah, Beverly Hills, the fancy place in all the movies and TV shows. Imagine, after growing up in poverty, I landed my first teaching job in an economically and socially upper-class school. Wow, talk about a contrast with what I grew up with. It was day and night, North Pole and South Pole.

I am very grateful that I had the experience of those schools. It was there I saw what all schools should be like and what all students should experience. In a perfect world, every school would have the resources those schools had. Furthermore, every school would have the expectations of kids that those schools had. There were only about eight Black kids there, out of a student body of 2,000. I felt like a sort of missionary. I realized that I was probably the first Black man that these students had ever experienced an intimate and respectful relationship with. I wasn't the gardener, or a servant, or a bus driver. I was their teacher. And I like to think that because of that, down the road, when those kids are running businesses and a Black man knocks at their door, they'll be better prepared to open it and see a fellow human being.

While I was physically in Beverly Hills, my heart and thoughts were fixed on other kids—kids who were like me, kids who weren't going to a top-flight high school and whose teachers didn't expect much from them. The students I longed to be among every day weren't the ones with all those resources and opportunities. I'll always remember one day when I was walking to my car after school and saw a white kid I knew. He said, "Hey, Mr. Fluker. Where are you going?" I said, "I'm going to my second job." (I always had another job while I was teaching there.) And he nodded and said, "Yeah, I'm going to my second school. Hebrew school." I asked, "What do you learn at Hebrew school?" and he said, "Aw, nothing. Just about how great my people are."

That hit me like a hammer. I was, like, wow. He was learning about his own people. Their history. Their legacy. His role in that larger group. What he owed to his ancestors. That's what the Jewish people do for their kids. And I thought, "That's the missing piece. We have to teach our kids that they have a legacy, too."

My heart longed so desperately to save children who were like me that I decided to leave Beverly Hills. When I said I was leaving our upscale high school to teach at Cleveland High School in Los Angeles, a lot of folks thought I should have my head examined. Cleveland was a Title I school, meaning that a lot of the students' families were poor. It was three times the size of the school I was coming from. I was taking a pay cut, and there were half a dozen gangs active there. But I figured, well, this is where I can make a difference. This is where I'm needed.

Things at Cleveland were pretty much as bad as I'd expected. In some ways they were worse. At the end of every year, we'd go through the process that schools all over America go through. The teachers would get together and the administrators would show us the school-wide achievement scores. The scores were broken down every kind of way—by class year, by gender, by race. Year after year, the African American students' scores got worse. Soon after I arrived at Cleveland, the scores for Black students were absolutely rock bottom—below the scores of ESL (English as a Second Language) students. Black kids were scoring lower than the students who didn't speak English!

Can you imagine how this hit us, we African American teachers? We'd sit in those meetings, looking at those scores, feeling embarrassed, angry, humiliated. And confused! Because we knew—I certainly knew—from my conversations with these kids that these scores were not a true representation of their intelligence. So why? Why??

At about this same time, Andre Chevalier, another Black teacher, was taking a master teaching class at the university. There he encountered a similar situation as the scores of African American students were flashed on the board. Being the only Black person in the room, he watched as every head swiveled and every eyeball fell on him, as if to say, "OK, you explain this."

That same night, Andre called me. He said. "Fluke, we have to do something." We met for lunch the next day. We called in another Black teacher, Bill Paden. I remember we kept saying, "This has to end right now."

So we went to our principal, Al Weiner. He's a Jewish guy, very progressive, very forward thinking. We said to him, "Al, we want to talk to the Black kids, alone. We have some things to say to them that you might want to say but you can't. We think we can."

Al had the guts to do what few school administrators would do. He said, "OK. Do what you think is best." He allowed us to start holding assemblies at the school that were for the Black kids only. The first assembly consisted of every Black person in the school. In addition to the 300-plus students, we had teachers, staff, lunch ladies, bus drivers, custodians. The adults formed a circle around the students. We showed them the test scores, and they were shocked. We talked to them as responsible parents talk to their children. We talked about our anger and frustration. We talked about our fears and our concerns. We talked about our love for them.

That was the beginning of what has grown into the Village Nation. The name is taken from an old African proverb, "It takes a village to raise a child." In a society where that village has been lost, we try to fill that gap. We, adults and students, have banded together in mutual caring and respect to raise each other up.

It's not always pretty. It's not all warm and fuzzy and group hugs. Raising children properly means telling them the truth, and the truth isn't always easy to hear. It means being really straight with a kid about how he's contributing to his own problems. But it's done in an atmosphere of love. Love equals discipline, and vice versa.

Going back to my story about the Jewish student going to Hebrew school—one of our priorities is educating kids about Black history. Not just the history of slavery, but their rich history as Kings and Queens. I'm astonished sometimes how little kids know about their own story. Not long ago I was walking down a hallway to give a lecture about the Jim Crow era. I stopped to talk to a young brother, and I dropped a book, which opened to a picture of a Ku Klux Klan member wearing the full getup—the sheet, the pointed hood, the whole thing. And the boy said, "What's that? Why's that fool wearing a hood?" I called a young sister over and showed her the same picture. She said, "Is it a Halloween thing?"

Can you imagine a Jewish seventeen-year-old not recognizing a swastika? Not knowing what it meant?

So I see a big part of our job as teaching our young people their story—the good and the bad.

Sometimes we are criticized for holding meetings that are for Black students only. I say that's crazy. The African American community is in crisis. Our kids are dying in the streets. They are incarcerated at record rates. We've lost one generation and are in the process of losing another. And you criticize me for segregating them for some honest talk? Are you kidding me? It's what any family would do. If you had three children, and one of your children was sick, and you stayed home to nurse that child, would that mean you didn't care about your other children? Of course not!

And that's what the Village Nation is—it's a family. Sometimes a family needs to do its dirty laundry, and you do it in private. You do it where it's safe. For instance, we Village elders travel around and do an assembly on the "N" word that is for Black students only. We talk about how the word evolved. How it was used to dehumanize Black people, making them subject to lynchings and other treatment that no one could justify doing to a human being. Today our young people are calling each other by that word—calling *themselves* by that word. We don't say to the kids, "We demand that you stop using this word." But we give them information and ask them to wrestle with the question, "Why would you use this word?" We would not hold that assembly with a mixed group. The tension would be too high. No one would feel safe— not the Black kids, not the other kids. It's like talking to a group of young girls about feminine hygiene. You wouldn't do that in a group that included boys. That kind of segregation isn't anti-white, or anti-Hispanic, or anti-anyone. It's about talking about things that need to be talked about in an atmosphere that's safe.

The Village Nation is in its fourth year now at Cleveland High School. And you know what? We have closed the achievement gap. *Closed* it. The first year of our existence, the African American kids' scores on the standard achievement tests rose 53 points. The scores are still climbing—this year, they're more than 140 points higher than they were when we began. In fact, the increase in scores was so dramatic that many schools and school districts want to know our secret. We boldly tell them, "Kids don't care what you know until they know that you care!"

After hearing about the success of the Village Nation, Bill Cosby and Oprah Winfrey have asked if we had anticipated our test scores shooting up. We replied that our focus was on the kids making better choices in all aspects of life. Improved test results have been only one of the many great byproducts of kids' good decision-making.

The Village Nation is about empowering the kids to make good decisions. Kids are always telling me, "I gotta do this, I gotta do that." I tell them, "No. What I've learned in my own life, what I want to pass on to you, is that the only thing you gotta do in life is die. Everything else is a choice, your choice. Beware, young brothers (and sisters), because all choices come with consequences. You have more power than you can possibly imagine—and your power lies in your choices."

Joseph Marshall, Jr.

About Joseph Marshall, Jr.

As Joe Marshall was growing up in South Central Los Angeles, he often heard his grandmother say, "The more you know, the more you owe." He wasn't sure what she meant.

But then he grew up and looked back at his life. Unlike many of his friends and acquaintances, he was raised in a strong, intact family. During the day his father dug ditches for a local utility company; at night his mother went to her job as a nurse. As Joe and his siblings grew, one parent was always there to offer support and discipline. Working together, the Marshalls managed to send all nine of their children to college.

Joe realized what an extraordinary gift his parents had given him. He accepted the idea that he owed it to his family to pass on that gift. He worked for years as a middle-school teacher, doing what he could to offer his students the kind of support he had received at home. But the problem was, he discovered, "At school, the bell always rings. But there's no bell on the street."

In order to touch more lives more effectively, Joe and a colleague, Jack Jacqua, founded the Omega Boys Club in San Francisco in 1987. Omega Boys Club is an organization aimed at teaching young people how to stay alive and free from violence while stressing academic achievement. Today Omega has seen more than 8,000 members graduate from high school or earn their GED, while more than 130 have graduated from college with the club's financial help. Joe Marshall and his organization have received an Oprah "Use Your Life" award and have been honored at the White House, given an *Essence* award, and profiled on network news programs. He is the host of the nationally syndicated radio program *Street Soldiers*.

Joseph Marshall, Jr. Speaks

If I had the chance to sit down with you and talk face to face, here are a few of the things I'd like to say.

I'd start out by saying it is really tough to be a kid today. I think it is especially tough to be a young Black male. There is so much stuff coming at you from different directions, and for many of you, 90 percent of that stuff is negative. All that stuff is programming you to fail. Let me say that again—you are being programmed to fail.

I run a club for boys called the Omega Boys Club, and I have a radio show called *Street Soldiers*. I meet young men who have just about everything in their lives steering them in the wrong direction. The streets are coming at them from every conceivable angle. They're being guided down the wrong path by their friends, their neighborhoods, their homes—even the music they listen to.

When I first meet a young man, he thinks I'm crazy. He's grown to be 15 (or 17 or 19 or whatever) believing that normal is abnormal and vice versa. He thinks it's normal to die at an early age. He thinks it's normal to go to jail. It's normal not to do well in school. It's normal not to graduate. It's normal to go to funerals for teenagers. It's normal not to have a father. It's normal to have a mother on drugs.

I have to tell him, "No, that's not normal. That is all abnormal." At first he doesn't believe me. Many young men—and maybe this applies to you—are so used to those conditions that they accept them. They accept the idea that they won't see 40. They accept the idea that prison and jail are in their future, the way other people accept the idea that they'll get their wisdom teeth.

It's always been hard to be a Black man in America. But it's harder now; oh yes, it's harder now. I call where we are now the "A.C. Era." A.C. means "After Crack."

Crack cocaine has changed everything.

There has always been a string of significant dates in Black American history. For instance, there's 1619, when the first African slaves arrived on these shores. There's the slavery era, the Civil War, the Emancipation Proclamation, the civil rights movement, and the Black power movement. Now, add 1980 to that list. That is about when crack cocaine entered the Black community. Crack cocaine, my God—it did something even slavery couldn't do. It did what the Ku Klux Klan couldn't do. And that is, it stopped the African American woman from mothering her children. Even in slavery times, mothers would take in other people's kids and care for them. Papa may have been a rolling stone, but Momma and Grandma were always there. They were the rocks of Gibraltar. They were the glue.

But crack put the men in jail and destroyed the mothers. It set the African American community back 100 years. Throughout our history in America, the one stable factor that allowed us Blacks to fight against whatever forces oppressed us was the family. Crack has destroyed that family structure. And our communities, neighborhoods, and larger society can only be as good as the families.

So that's where the Omega Boys Club and the

Joseph Marshall, Jr.

Street Soldiers radio show come in. We are much less programs than we are a family. We step into the gap, trying to provide the structure that a healthy, functioning family would provide.

So maybe you're thinking, "Well, great, but Omega Boys Club is in San Francisco. What good can that do me?" I really wish I could be in your town and hear your story and talk to you personally. But I truly believe that my years of experience can give you some tools to help yourself. Let me tell you a little more about how I see young men who are walking on a self-destructive path and how I try to intercede with them. You can internalize what you read here and apply it to your own life. You can even spread it to those around you.

If you're caught up in the "abnormal as normal" mindset, you may be used to people seeing you as a bad kid, an evil kid, a kid who just doesn't care. You may even feel some pressure to live up to those labels. I don't see you that way, because I think we're dealing with a health problem here. Yeah, a health problem. You've been infected—infected with a faulty mindset. That doesn't make you bad. I'm fighting the flu right now myself. Does that make me bad? No! I just got infected and got sick. But in too many cases we say to infected kids, "You're bad, you're worthless, go to jail." And what happens when they go to jail? They meet other infected people, and they get worse. They never get treated for what ails them, so they just do the same things over and over. We can build all the prisons we want, but that won't change anything. Prisons are not the hospitals for the sickness we're dealing with.

How do kids get infected in the first place? They get infected through bad advice, bad information, bad examples. The sneaky thing is that this bad advice doesn't look bad. In fact, it looks like what everybody wants—survival skills. It usually comes from some older person in the hood who seems to know the score. He might say to you, "I'm gonna help you. It's rough out here; you gotta know how to survive." Well, any animal wants to survive, right? So you hear that word and it's like, BING, yeah, tell me. Then you hear, "You gotta handle your business. Don't be no punk. Get your respect. Get your money on. Don't let nobody disrespect you. You gotta carry a gun. You gotta sell dope."

Usually there's some tiny germ of truth at the center—like "Stand up for yourself." OK, that can be good advice. But the other stuff attached to it is completely bullshit. It's packaged as survival skills, but it's nothing of the kind. That kind of advice won't help you survive; it'll only help you die. Somebody looking at it from the outside can see it's crazy, deadly stuff, but if you're surrounded by that talk 24/7 . . .

I'll give you an example. I say to the young men at the club, "What's 2 + 2?" They say, "4." I say, "No it's not. It's 5." They laugh. But I say, "What if your mother told you it was 5? What if all the OG's in the street said it was 5? What if they'd been telling you it was 5 as long as you could remember? You'd believe them, right?" It's the same principle. You've been told that if you do these things, you'll come out on top, you will survive. But look around you. Are the people who are living by those rules surviving? Are they living well? You can see they aren't. They're the same ones whose funerals you're going to. They're filling up prison cells. And yet you hang on to the idea that 2 + 2 is 5. Maybe the people who told you that really believed it. You can have well-intentioned people giving you bad information. But their good intentions don't change the fact that it's bad information.

So if I were meeting you today, and I saw that you had been programmed for death and incarceration, I would do what I could to pull that programming out of you. I'd try to help you unlearn the abnormal, risk-taking behaviors that you may believe are normal.

If you've learned that carrying a gun is normal, that using language that provokes violence is normal, that putting material values over people is normal, that seeing women in a negative light is normal, that using and selling drugs is normal—I'd tell you, "No, son. Those are *not* normal. Let me pull those behaviors out of you."

And then what?

I'd give you something better to put in those behaviors' place. I'd say, "Let me give you some rules to live by that will decrease the chance of your becoming a perpetrator or a victim of violence. These rules will steer you back onto the right track." I'd tell you the truth—I have never lost a young person who genuinely lives by these rules.

Time would be short. So I'd give you only two rules. The first and most essential rule is something you can take and use right now.

A friend will never lead you into danger.

And here's an important corollary to that rule: *A gang member cannot be your friend.*

I can hear you telling me, like a thousand young men have told me before, "What are you talking about? He's my homie! He's got my back! I can talk to him!"

I say no. If you think that a gang member is

your friend, it is because you don't understand what friendship is.

Think about it. Say you're in a gang with your "friends." If you decide you want to leave the gang, what do they say to you? They say, "I'll kill you."

These are your friends and they're going to kill you?

It's a very simple test. A true friend will never put you in danger.

Danger should be your filter for everything and everybody.

I have a little exercise I'd like you to do. Write down the names of everybody you call your friends, your family, your loved ones. Then go through that list and beside every name, write "S" for Safe or "D" for Dangerous.

I wish I could see your list. If it's like a lot of lists I look at, I'd see maybe 20 names. Maybe two of those names are marked "S" and 18 are marked "D."

And still, the kids who make those lists try to tell me, "Bullets don't have no names on them," or "Anyone can be in the wrong place at the wrong time," or "It can happen to anyone." I'm telling you, that is bull. YOU'RE AROUND 18 DANGEROUS PEOPLE! That is why something bad is going to happen to you. Your danger quotient is 90 percent! It's not the neighborhood you live in—it's the PEOPLE you're associating with!

A friend will never lead you into danger. Memorize that. Live by it. Your chances of survival have just increased enormously.

OK, here's a second rule I want to leave with you today.

Change begins from within.

Remember I was talking before about having the flu? I've been sick for three weeks. But I'm getting better. You know why? I went to my doctor. He gave me a prescription for medication. He told me some things to do to take care of myself. But that's all he can do. He's didn't go with me to the pharmacy to pick up the medicine. He doesn't come to my house at 10 p.m. to remind me to take that pill.

You see what I'm saying? The prescription absolutely works. But it's only good if I take it. Nobody else can do that for me.

But when a young man with his life ahead of him takes the prescription—takes the responsibility for changing his life from within—damn, there's no stopping him.

Let me tell you real quickly about one kid. His

name is Andre, and I first met him in the streets of Oakland when he was 17. He'd had a hard time when he was younger. He was picked on because he was a short guy and he was smart and a good student. One day a friend of his father's told him, "Don't let them punk you. You gotta fight." So he went to school and went nuts on the guys who were hassling him. He fought them. And suddenly instead of being picked on, he was getting all these props. It was, "Hey lil' cousin. You need anything?"

So soon he was fighting every day, skipping school, doing all this stuff because along with the germ of truth about standing up for himself, he had bought the whole package. And a few years later there he was on the street, selling drugs and gangbanging and headed for prison and an early death.

When I came along and started telling Dre what I knew, and he started coming over to the club, it was such a beautiful thing. It was so much fun reeling that kid in. To make a long story short, he went back for his GED, then college, and he ended up teaching at the school he was kicked out of. He was an assistant principal for ten years. Now he's back here working with me at the Boys Club. He's my operations manager, my second in command. He's married and has two kids—he's no baby daddy; he's a husband and father. He's the most moral person I've ever met.

Every kid is Dre. There is so much good in them. And there is so much good in you.

We're in hard times, here in the A.C. Era. But you know what we're involved in, you and me? We're in a marathon relay race, going through the breadth of Black history. I'm looking back to all the people who came before me, back to the pharaohs in Egypt, through Frederick Douglass, and Martin Luther King, and Malcolm X, and Paul Robeson. They've been passing the baton on for generations, and now it's come to me. I owe all those people. If it hadn't been for them, I wouldn't be here having the chance to do what I'm doing. I'm handing on the baton to each of the young men I'm reaching. I hope you'll pick it up and run the race of your life.